IMAGES

A WORKBOOK FOR ENHANCING SELF-ESTEEM AND PROMOTING CAREER PREPARATION, ESPECIALLY FOR BLACK GIRLS

By Mattie Evans Gray

Designed and illustrated by
Dalia Visgirda

Developed by the
CIRCLE PROJECT
California State University, Sacramento

For the
California State Department of Education

1

Publishing Information

Images: A Workbook for Enhancing Self-esteem and Promoting Career Preparation, Especially for Black Girls, which was written by Mattie Evans Gray, was produced by the CIRCLE Project, California State University, Sacramento, for the California State Department of Education. Hortense E. Thornton is the director of the CIRCLE Project. For a list of others who contributed to this document, see pages 182 and 183. The development of *Images* was funded under the provisions of Public Law 98-524, the Carl Perkins Vocational Education Act of 1984, as administered by the Career-Vocational Preparation Division in the State Department of Education. However, the points of view and opinions expressed in this document do not necessarily reflect the position or policies of the State Department or the federal government, and no official endorsement should be inferred. It is important to note that no person shall, on the grounds of sex, race, color, national origin, age, or handicap, be excluded from participation in, be denied the benefits of, or be subjected to discrimination under any program supported in whole or in part by PL 98-524.

Images was published by the California State Department of Education, 721 Capitol Mall, Sacramento, California (mailing address: P.O. Box 944272, Sacramento, CA 94244-2720). It was printed by the Office of State Printing and distributed under the provisions of the Library Distribution Act.

Copies of this publication are available for $6 each, plus sales tax for California residents, from the Bureau of Publications, Sales Unit, California State Department of Education, P.O. Box 271, Sacramento, CA 95802-0271.

A list of other publications available from the Department of Education may be found at the end of this document, or a complete list may be obtained by writing to the address cited above or by calling the Bureau of Publications: (916) 445-1260.

ISBN 0-8011-0782-2

Contents

Preface

The future holds many opportunities and challenges for you. No matter what direction your life takes, you can be sure that the only person you will always have is you. Therefore, you must begin now your preparation to become a responsible and self-sufficient adult. You must set goals for the future and prepare to take control of your life. Your workbook can serve as a guide to help you set career and life goals.

We wish we could tell you of some shortcuts or some easy ways to achieve success and economic security, but we cannot. However, we can tell you that an important first step toward becoming self-sufficient is to acquire knowledge about yourself and the world around you. Stay in school and obtain the education and the training needed to develop your potential. Then your journey will be easier all along the way.

JAMES T. ALLISON
State Director
of Career-Vocational Preparation
California State Department
of Education

CONSTANCE F. GIPSON
Consultant, Vocational
Education Gender Equity

Foreword

The world is constantly changing, and California is no exception. One must have a firm sense of identity as well as a sense of one's place in this world. *Images* can help you accomplish that goal. The exercises in this workbook are designed to help you identify your strengths and weaknesses in order to develop your full potential. The women presented as role models in *Images* are a diverse group; however, women all stress the value of education, self-discipline, motivation, and assertiveness as essential in achieving goals.

The following successful women, who are featured in *Images,* possess the qualities needed to become a success in today's world: Rosamond Bolden, Manager; Alice A. Lytle, Municipal Court Judge; Tia Hunnicut, Dollmaker; Josephine Richardson, Security Company Owner; Pamela Spearman, Design Engineer; Caroline Ledbetter, Physicist; Pauline Campbell, Equipment Planning Manager; Daphne L. Rhoe, Telecommunications Systems Manager; Celestine Y. Farmon, Superintendent; Norma Sklarek, Architect; Monique T. Godbold, Chemical Engineer; Linda Tanner, Stationary Engineer; Valerie Weir, Electronics Technician; Arlene Stevens, Television Program Director; Monica Crooks, General Dentist; Alicia K. Dixon, Public Health Trainee; Lillian Brown, Police Officer; LaRuth McReynolds, Administrative Law Judge; Donna M. Smith, College Dean; Donnette D. Chatters, Telecommunications Analyst; and Joanne Lewis, University Administrator.

California is a state in transition. As Deputy Superintendent of Specialized Programs for the State Department of Education, my visitations to schools throughout the state have convinced me of the importance of aligning academic counseling with career and vocational preparation to meet the needs of young Black females in order to prepare for their future.

I applaud the efforts of Constance Gipson, a consultant with the State Department of Education, in organizing an outstanding advisory committee that represented diversity in the educational community. Noteworthy were the contributions of the support staff in compiling and marketing the book.

Images opens the door for lifetime options, where an individual can choose a career of choice from a wide variety of future job opportunities.

It is a privilege to release this outstanding book to schools in the state of California. The task is for educators to prepare young Black females for jobs in the future. *Images* is an excellent tool to be used by educators in this endeavor.

Best wishes for a successful future.

SHIRLEY A. THORNTON
Deputy Superintendent
Specialized Programs Branch

Introduction

IMAGES is a very special book. It is different from all other books because it is a book for you, about you. Everything in this book focuses on you: your self-awareness, your future career, your future life-style. As you think about yourself and write in your book, you are going to answer these important questions:

WHO AM I?   WHERE AM I GOING?   HOW DO I GET THERE?

Because these questions are so important, a number of women who live and work in California speak to you from the pages of your book and share their answers. Some of these women were very much like you when they were in school, so you can learn from them about opportunities and resources that you may rely on to achieve your academic and career goals.

WHO AM I?

In Chapter One you explore your attitudes, feelings, values, and interests. You learn more about how your African-American heritage influences your ideas and behavior. You also identify important people in your life and develop your own family tree. Taking a close look at yourself helps you become more aware of your personal power and potential to achieve academically and socially.

You continue to build on what you already know about yourself in Chapter Two. You gain a better understanding of how you communicate with people and why they may sometimes misunderstand or disagree with you. You also learn more about your language behavior as you examine how you would respond in several situations.

Chapter Three introduces you to the world of work. You increase your self-awareness by identifying your work habits and work values. You also discover that already you have a place in the world of work. In this chapter you focus attention on how the skills you are developing in school can affect your future success in the job market.

WHERE AM I GOING?

In Chapter Four you review your school experiences and make a record of classes and activities that are helping you to develop skills in eight competency areas. You also identify barriers that may sometimes interfere with your academic progress, and you decide how to overcome these barriers. A make-believe trip into your future highlights the relationship between your academic performance and your career plans.

You explore career options in Chapter Five. By matching your skills, interests, and work values with various occupations, you learn more about career choices that may be just right for you. You also meet a number of role models who are achieving success in reaching their career and life goals.

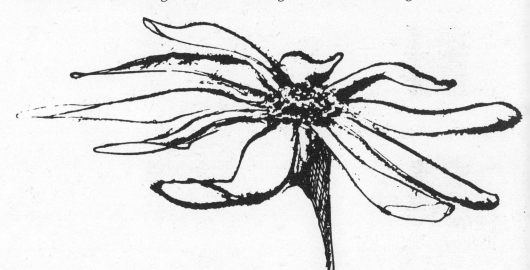

HOW DO I GET THERE?

In Chapter Six you gain a greater awareness of how personal decisions can prevent you from reaching academic or career goals. You also examine your attitudes toward marriage and parenthood and gain some insights about the responsibilities you will face as an adult.

In Chapter Seven you summarize what you learned about yourself and your relationships with people and what you learned from the role models. You develop your own definitions of success, set goals for the future, and develop plans for reaching those goals. The knowledge you gain by completing your book enables you to answer the question: Who am I? Your awareness of who you are provides the basic foundation you need for building self-esteem and for making decisions about your future career and life-style.

PART I

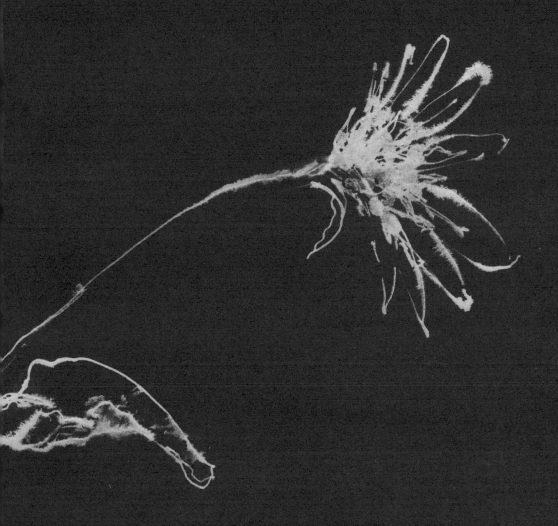

Who Am I?

You were born with innate value and a purpose for your life. Because you are a child of the universe, it is natural for you to grow and develop. Just as a living plant grows toward the sun, you strive to grow and mature — to reach your full potential as a person.

Chapter One

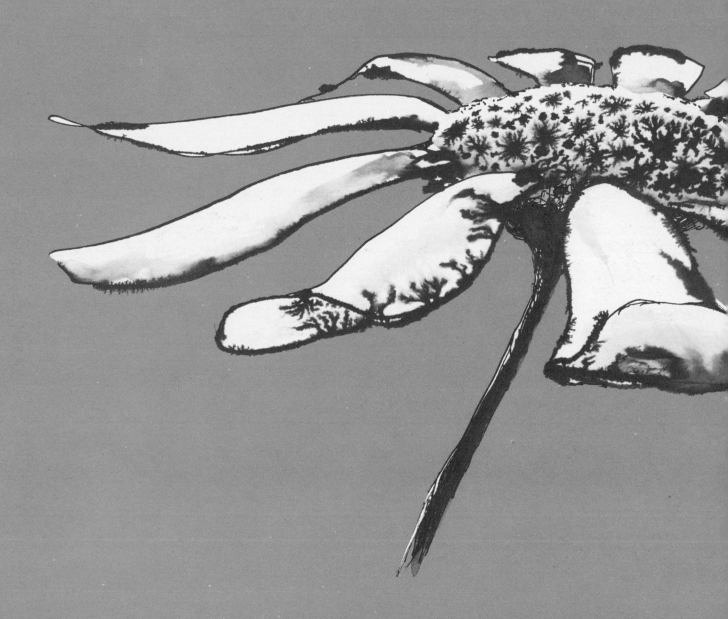

listen children
keep this in the place
you have for keeping
always
keep it all ways

we have never hated black

listen
we have been ashamed
hopeless   tired   mad
but always
all ways
we loved us

we have always loved each other
children   all ways

pass it on

                    – Lucille Clifton
        from *Good News About the Earth*

THE SEARCH FOR SELF

    Before you begin your search for self, you must have some
knowledge of your beginnings. This knowledge provides you with a
sense of history and a feeling that you belong. Awareness of who
you are is a foundation to build on as you look toward the future
and make decisions about what you want to achieve in life.

African Heritage

Many years of painstaking research and discoveries have led to one focal point as the place where human life began—Africa's Great Rift Valley. There are many questions yet unanswered by scientists and scholars, but little doubt remains that civilization began in Africa.

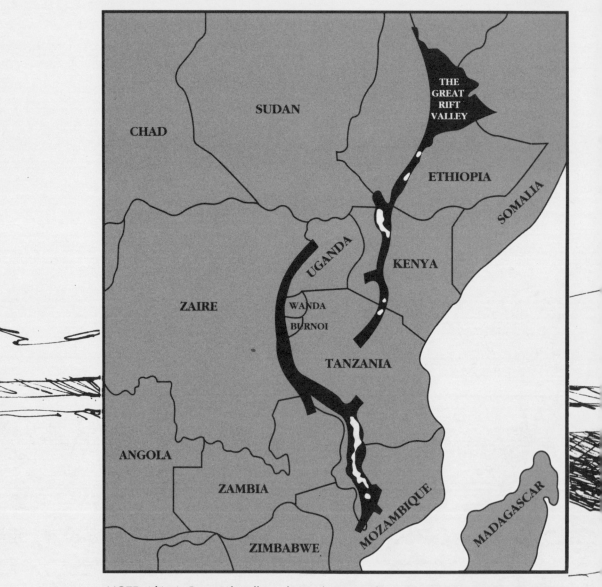

NOTE: Africa's Great Rift Valley is located in East Africa. Louis S.B. Leakey, anthropologist, found fossil remains that were believed to be heading toward modern man. See *National Geographic,* November, 1966: 701-706.

That vast continent is beautiful and rich in untapped resources. Nevertheless, survival there has always been difficult. During centuries of growth and change, African people learned how to adapt to their natural environment so that they could not only survive but also set up great kingdoms and empires.

Before the development of efficient methods of producing crops and livestock, the food supply consisted of whatever animals and plants nature provided. The people remained in an area until they used up the available food sources; then they moved on to another location to hunt and gather food.

The people of Africa lived in kinship groups also known as tribes. A tribe is a group of people who share common ancestry, language, and customs. A sense of solidarity made each tribe feel protected from outsiders. Because they were forced to move from place to place to find new food supplies, the various tribes often came in contact with one another. Sometimes this contact led to conflicts. In order to resolve conflicts and to maintain group solidarity, each tribe developed its own rules or laws and customs. The customs were rules of conduct based on the beliefs of the group and were taught to the children so that they would know how to behave. There were laws and customs for marriage, family life, property rights, religion, wealth, and politics.

African laws and customs were based on the belief that human life, plant life, animal life, and mineral life were valuable elements of nature. These natural elements constantly influenced one another and each existed for a purpose. The people believed that it was important to have proper respect for all elements of nature and to use them wisely.

Within each tribe there were numerous extended families made up of relatives and friends who shared mutual concern for one another. All family members were expected to live by a set of moral standards for right and wrong.

Those who violated the morals received strong disapproval. The moral standards, no doubt, had a positive influence on family life.

Generally, family ties were strong; close relationships existed between mothers and children. Mothers were highly respected because they passed on the heritage. In other words, they taught their children the beliefs, customs, and values of the family. For example, children were taught that they must show respect for the age and wisdom of the elderly. The knowledge that was passed on by the mothers made it easier for the children to behave in ways that would gain them approval from the family and the tribe.

Discipline, mutual support, and cooperation made it possible for families to function economically. All family members—females, males, children, adults—had their roles. They were expected to work and carry out their responsibilities according to the division of labor. The division of labor was an arrangement in which tasks were distributed so that all family members had specific jobs. This system made it possible for families to produce more than they needed. As a result, they could trade for things that they did not produce themselves. This mutual cooperation provided families with basic necessities and the potential for accumulating wealth.

The women of Africa played many roles—mother, agricultural worker, trader, warrior, and queen. In these roles they could enjoy high social and economic status. Agricultural workers, for example, were allowed to keep what they earned. Women who were skilled in crafts gained wealth as a result of trading their products. Those who were queens controlled vast wealth and power. In general, African women were actively involved in the economic and political life of their tribes.

A heritage of strong family ties, independence, and active participation in the division of labor provided a basis for the entry of African women into American society and into the American labor force.

As you explore and learn more about who you are, it is important for you to remember that you are connected to your African-American heritage. Your unique cultural heritage includes customs, ideas, values, art, music, literature, and material objects. Knowledge of your heritage will help you grow toward your potential.

NOTE: American labor force refers to workers, paid and unpaid, whose services contributed to the American economy. The first Black women who came to America entered the labor force immediately as indentured servants, paid workers, or as slaves, unpaid workers.

AFRICAN-AMERICAN VALUES

The following are some of the values that are a part of your cultural heritage. Rely on these values to guide your decisions and behavior.

APPROPRIATENESS - There are accepted rules for personal conduct. Once you learn these rules you know how to behave, especially in new or confusing situations.

RESPECT - Love and respect yourself so that you will be able to respect others and their rights. Self-respect enables you to be in control of your behavior.

KNOWLEDGE - Knowledge about yourself, your social environment, and the choices available to you provide you with a sense of power. Knowledge will enable you to make wise choices and give you some control over the situations that will occur in your life.

EXCELLENCE - It is important to strive to be your best and to do your best in all things. Achievement results in a sense of self-worth.

ADAPTABILITY - It is sometimes necessary to adjust to unexpected events. Family situations may require you to take on the roles and responsibilities of other family members. Mutual responsibility strengthens the family unit and also allows you to develop your potential.

RESTRAINT - Your sense of self-worth, along with family values and rules, will enable you to exercise control over your behavior and decisions. The ability to set limits on yourself will increase your self-esteem and help you reach your personal goals.

NOTE: African-American values are emphasized in order to provide a connection to the student's cultural heritage. These values, of course, may be similar to those of other cultural groups in America. The values are adapted from Wade Nobles, "Reconstructing the Black Family," Sex-Equity Mini-Conference, Los Angeles, January 23, 1987.

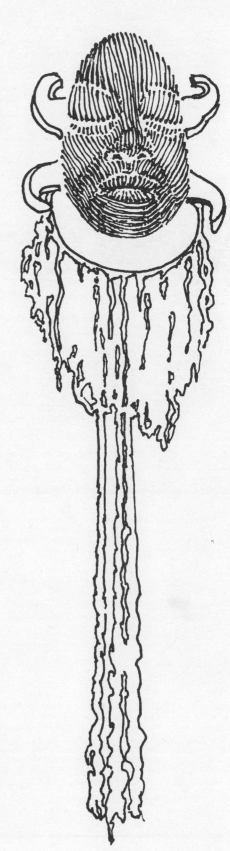

Who Am I?

The search for your own identity is a lifelong process. You are continually developing and trying to understand yourself. Although it may be frustrating at times, you need to continue to seek answers to the question Who am I? The answers must make sense to you.

As you were growing up, relatives and friends provided for your care and taught you the basic language and behavior patterns that you needed to know in order to get along as a member of the family. You learned that you were a real person and that it was important for you to be recognized by others. Even if you did not receive all of the attention that you thought you deserved, someone taught you what you needed to know in order for you to be where you are now.

At this stage in your life, you have in your mind a collection of thoughts, feelings, and ideas about yourself. This collection is what is known as the *self-concept*. As you continue your search for self, you will discover talents, skills, and aptitudes that you need to develop. Your concept of self will eventually include not only "who I am" but also "what I can do."

From time to time you evaluate yourself and make judgments about the kind of person you are. The feelings that you have about yourself make up your *self-esteem*. Your feelings are influenced by other people such as relatives, friends, and teachers. Sometimes the experiences you have with others make you feel good about yourself. At other times, the experiences you have may cause you not to feel good about yourself. Your self-esteem varies according to the situation that you are in or the people you are with at a given time.

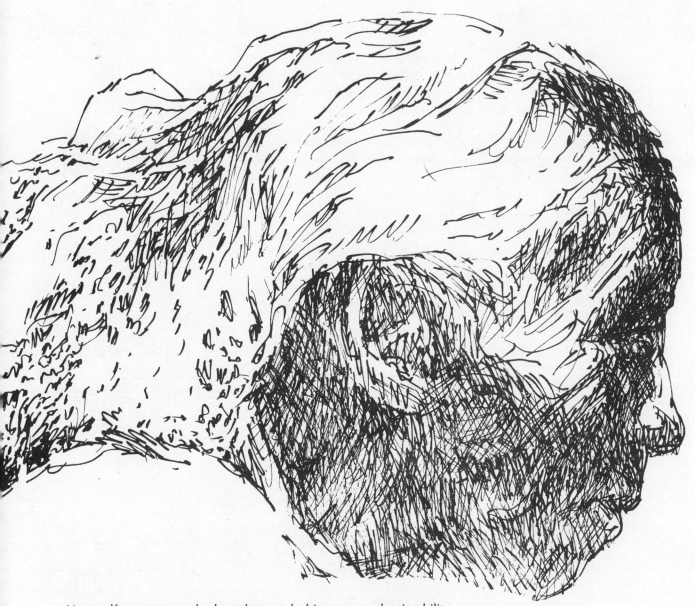

Your self-esteem may be based on such things as academic ability, speaking ability, athletic ability, or dress and physical appearance. Because you are free to make choices, you can take an active role in building your self-esteem. You can put your time and energy into activities and social relationships that make you feel good about yourself.

Your ability to choose to act in a certain way makes you responsible for your decisions and behavior and for the results of your choices. Before making a decision you can look at the alternatives and decide how you want to behave. Thus you can take an active role in creating the kind of person you want to be.

My Family Tree

ME

Extended family: a group of relatives and friends who provide emotional and economic support for one another. Although all family members do not all reside in the same household, they share responsibility for the care and rearing of the children. There is a strong emphasis on respect for elders because they provide stability and wisdom. Loyalty and cooperation strengthen the bonds between family members. For many, religion plays an important role because it provides hope and comfort, especially during times of crisis.

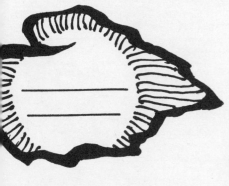

People Close to Me and How I Feel About Them

This tree represents your extended family—people who have guided and supported you as you have been growing toward maturity. Some of them have been relatives; some have been friends, teachers, or people in your community.

Write your name in the center circle above the word "me."
In each circle write on the top line the name of a person in your
extended family. On the line below the name, write a word that describes that
person.

MY EXTENDED FAMILY AND ME

Write about your feelings toward the people in your family tree. How have these people influenced your life? Why are they important to you? Why do you think you are important to them?

_____

_____

_____

_____

_____

_____

_____

_____

_____

_____

_____

_____

Someone else's legs do you no good in traveling.
- African Proverb

My Personal Values

You are constantly making decisions about what to do and what to say. The choices that you make are based on the values you have learned from your family and other influences in your environment. Your personal values reflect what you think is important and what has meaning in your life.

From the list below choose five values and tell why each is important to you. Space is provided for you to include other values that are not listed.

- Making good grades
- Approval of friends
- Not going along with the crowd
- Being given an equal chance
- Having good friends
- Freedom to make my own decisions
- Having a relationship with a boy
- Having people respect me
- Being involved in religious activities
- Being needed by others
- Honesty from my parents
- Being able to like myself
- Being independent
- Getting along with parents

- Knowledge about the world I live in
- Loyalty from my friends
- Remaining a virgin until marriage
- Having lots of money
- Getting a good education
- Having a healthy body
- Helping others
- Honesty from my friends
- Having privacy
- Other:_____
- _____
- _____
- _____

I VALUE
_____

_____

_____

_____

_____

I VALUE
_____

_____

_____

_____

_____

I VALUE
_____

_____

_____

_____

_____

I VALUE
_____

_____

_____

_____

_____

I VALUE
_____

_____

_____

_____

_____

Exploring Attitudes and Interests

Another way to learn more about yourself is to explore your attitudes and interests. An attitude is a feeling that may cause you to act a certain way. An interest is something you like or something that appeals to you.

Think about your behavior, feelings, likes, and dislikes; then complete each of the following statements.

•*A happy time for me was* _____

_____

•*When I am twenty-five years old,* _____

_____

•*I am good at* _____

_____

•*If a friend asks me to skip a class,* _____

_____

•*When I hurt someone's feelings,* _____

_____

•*I wish my teachers would* _____

_____

•*I get angry when* _____

_____

•*I do my best work when teachers* _____

_____

•*When someone hurts my feelings, I* _____

_____

•*In school I do my best when* _____

_____

•*I admire adults who* _____

_____

•*People close to me think I am* _____

_____

•*When I have trouble talking to my parents,* _____

_____

•*I feel loved most when* _____

_____

•*It's hard for me to deal with* _____

_____

•*I am discouraged by a teacher who* _____

_____

•*My friends can count on me to* _____

_____

•*When I'm alone, I like to* _____

_____

•*What I want most in life is* _____

_____

•*I have never liked* _____

_____

•*My greatest strength is* _____

_____

•*I need to improve most in* _____

_____

•*When people meet me the first time, they* _____

_____

•*If I become a parent, I* _____

_____

•*Someday I am going to* _____

_____

Images: Messages from the Media

Some of your ideas about yourself are learned from television, radio, movies, and magazines. More than you realize, your thoughts and behavior are influenced by messages from the media. Sometimes the messages are indirect, just slight hints; sometimes the messages are very direct. Either way, they can be quite powerful. As you know, commercials can get your attention in just a few seconds and convince you to buy a product. They are designed to make you think that you need what is being advertised.

Frequently, media images portray fantasy instead of reality. For example, you are given the impression that success comes without any effort. Programs about rich and famous people highlight their expensive cars, elegant mansions, and fine clothes. The programs often fail to explain that it takes years of training, hard work, and personal sacrifices to get and to keep those things.

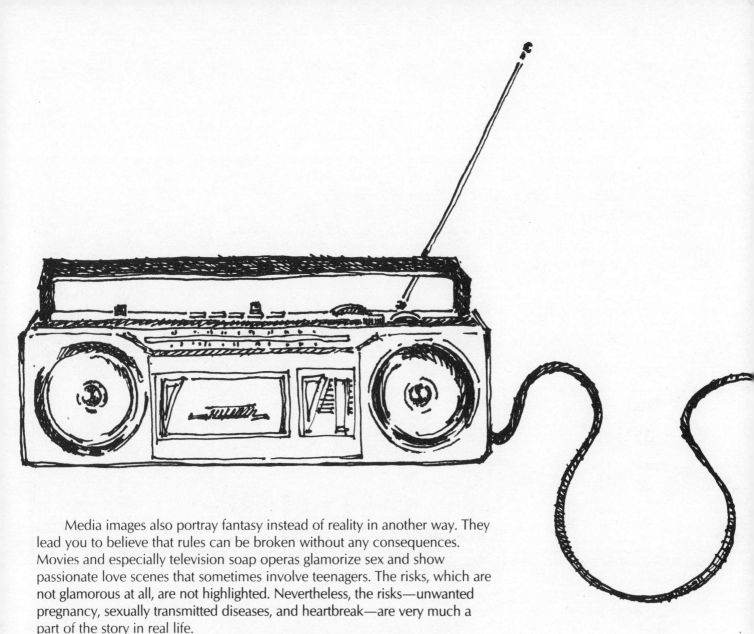

Media images also portray fantasy instead of reality in another way. They lead you to believe that rules can be broken without any consequences. Movies and especially television soap operas glamorize sex and show passionate love scenes that sometimes involve teenagers. The risks, which are not glamorous at all, are not highlighted. Nevertheless, the risks—unwanted pregnancy, sexually transmitted diseases, and heartbreak—are very much a part of the story in real life.

Sometimes media images devalue females and suggest that women neither think nor make decisions; they can merely look pretty. For example, magazine ads designed to sell cars or beverages frequently use pictures of females in revealing gowns or bathing suits to help sell the products. The hidden message is that only men make decisions about what to buy. What better way to get their attention than to use an appealing picture. Such practices treat females as objects and also ignore the fact that they, too, make decisions about which products to buy.

Many of the media images that you are exposed to are culturally inaccurate because they present an imbalanced view of African-American culture. For example, television tends to portray Black females as either lazy and dependent or pushy and domineering. Although these descriptions do not fit the majority of Black females, images that depict them as intelligent, efficient, and cooperative are practically absent from the television screen. Therefore, viewers are left to assume that Black females with these characteristics do not exist. Television has a strong influence on people's opinions. People tend to believe that what they see on the television screen is true.

The media do present, however, images that are positive and factual as well as entertaining. Listening to music, reading books and magazines, and viewing television can be both enjoyable and educational. What you are exposed to depends a great deal on the choices that you make. You are free to choose what you want to read and what you want to view and hear. It is important to be selective, however, so that you can be exposed to realistic images and positive role models.

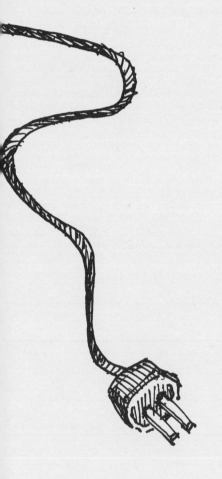

MESSAGES I GET FROM THE MEDIA:

•My favorite television program is _____

because _____

_____

_____

•Three women on television whom I admire; how their personalities and behavior impress me.

1. _____

_____

_____

2. _____

_____

_____

3. _____

_____

_____

•Two commercials I like and why I like them:

1. _____

2. _____

•Two movies I like and why I like them:

1. _____

2. _____

•My favorite singer is _____

because _____

_____

_____

•Two songs I like and why I like them:

1. _____

_____

2. _____

_____

•Magazines that I read regularly are _____

_____

•I like to read about _____

_____

•A book I have read for pleasure during the past year is _____

•What impressed me about that book _____

_____

_____

Personal Power: Self-control

As you continue your growth toward maturity, you will realize that you have personal power—**a sense of self-worth and confidence in your ability to make decisions**. Personal power enables you to resist peer pressure and helps you to overcome barriers that make it difficult for you to develop your talents and abilities. You can resist peer pressure and barriers because you know that you have the right to grow toward your full potential.

Earlier in this chapter you learned about a set of values that are a part of your African-American heritage. These values can support you as you assert your personal power.

Excellence - Striving to be your best will strengthen your sense of self-worth.

Appropriateness - Knowing the rules for behavior in various situations will prevent you from having to rely on your peers for direction.

Knowledge - Knowledge will help you to make wise choices and will give you more control over situations that will occur in your life.

Restraint - Your ability to set limits on your behavior will help you reach personal goals.

Adaptability - Your ability to adapt to changes and unexpected events will help to open doors of opportunity.

Respect - Your sense of self-respect enables you to be in control of your behavior at all times.

The Motivation to Achieve

Through trial and error you have learned how to do many things. You have discovered that if you are willing to try, you can learn a new skill or complete a task successfully. Your willingness to try comes from the feeling that you can do well enough to satisfy yourself and other people.

MOTIVATION:
Your inner desire to learn, to perform a task,
to create things—to **ACHIEVE**.

The motivation to achieve is not given to you at school. It is your own sense of personal power that provides you with the confidence you need to achieve.

WHY DO YOU WANT TO ACHIEVE?

When you complete a task, you gain a personal reward—a sense of satisfaction that your willingness to try has paid off for you. As you continue to try and in return get satisfactory results, your pride and self-esteem increase. Your self-confidence also increases; therefore, when you attempt a new or difficult task, you are willing to try again and again until you get the desired results.

Sometimes when you achieve or perform a task, you gain recognition and approval from other people, such as parents, friends, and teachers. In fact, it is very important for you to have others recognize your achievements and then let you know they approve by rewarding you. Their rewards may vary from a smile or pat on the back to a grade or a valuable gift. Nevertheless, what others think of you and how they react to what you do greatly influence your desire to achieve. Just remember that you must achieve because **you want to realize your potential**.

HOW DO YOU ACHIEVE?

SOCIAL ACHIEVEMENT:

The use of your skills and abilities to communicate with people and get along with them.

THE DESIRE TO GET ALONG . . .

Social achievement occurs when you associate with your peers, family members, teachers, or others in the school setting. You are constantly using your skills to express your ideas and feelings so that others will respond in a manner that is acceptable to you.

ACADEMIC ACHIEVEMENT:

The use of your skills and abilities to acquire knowledge and to perform tasks related to learning.

THE DESIRE TO ACHIEVE . . .

Academic achievement occurs when you acquire knowledge or perform tasks that help you develop your skills. You learn at home as well as at school. Hobbies, homework, games, and family celebrations are learning activities that help to improve your academic performance at school.

Both social achievement and academic achievement provide you with personal satisfaction as well as recognition and rewards from others. Satisfactory achievement in both areas contributes to your self-esteem. Therefore, it is important to maintain a balance between the two. Whenever a conflict occurs between your desire to get along and your desire to learn, rely on your values and sense of personal power to help you make the decisions needed to maintain the proper balance.

ACHIEVEMENT PATTERNS:

Review the definitions of SOCIAL ACHIEVEMENT and ACADEMIC ACHIEVEMENT. Think about your behavior and activities. Then list some of them under each of the headings. Next to the item place a check under ME if you gain personal satisfaction. Place a check under OTHERS if you gain recognition/reward from others. You may need to check both spaces for some items.

SOCIAL ACHIEVEMENT	ME	OTHERS	ACADEMIC ACHIEVEMENT	ME	OTHERS
play in the band	x	x	good at listening		x

Review your lists and ask yourself these questions:

•Do I achieve more in one area (academic or social) than the other? _____

•Are my academic achievements related more to school subjects or to extracurricular activities? _____

_____

•Do I achieve more for myself or for others? _____

Write a paragraph that tells what you have learned about your motivation to achieve.

_____

_____

_____

_____

_____

_____

_____

_____

_____

Reading for Pleasure

Although your structured school schedule demands that you concern yourself with many requirements, you can still set aside time to read for pleasure. Pleasurable reading can be not only enjoyable but also inspirational and help you understand more about yourself and the complex world in which you are growing up.

If you like reading about historical figures, *Black Foremothers: Three Lives* by Dorothy Sterling is a must. In this book, you will meet Ellen Craft, a runaway slave who became a great antislavery leader; Ida B. Wells, an investigative journalist and lecturer against the crime of lynching; and Mary Church Terrell, a dedicated leader in the movements for women's voting rights and civil rights.

You will be rewarded wonderfully by the poetry of Lucille Clifton, a very special poet who lives in California, and who speaks directly to you in her poem, which appears at the beginning of this book. She writes in a simple language which celebrates the Black family and youth. Of her writing style and subjects, she says the following:

> My style and my content stem from my experience. I grew up a well-loved child in a loving family, and so I have always known that being very poor, which we were, had nothing to do with lovingness or familyness or character or any of that. . . . when I write, especially for children, I try to get that across: that being poor or whatever your circumstances, you are capable of being the best of people and that best, as a human, does not come from the outside in, it comes from the inside out.

You are certain to enjoy reading poems from her books *Good Times, Good News About the Earth*, and *Generations*.

The novels of Joyce Carol Thomas, another writer who lives in California, should prove appealing to you. In *Marked by Fire, Bright Shadow,* and *Water Girl,* you will follow the life of Abyssinia Jackson, as well as meet several generations of remarkable Black women and men who live in rural America and are firmly rooted in their African heritage. Joyce Carol Thomas has clear ideas about her readers as the following comment demonstrates:

> I love to tickle the curiosity of young adults, to compel my readers to journey beyond their home towns with me and sample the lives of others within the secure adventure of the traveled page. If they have spent a pleasant time finding a new friend, feeling what the main character feels—loving, frowning, grieving, joking, weeping—I have created another world for these young readers in which they may walk in other settings, talk with new neighbors, and breathe inside other skins.

Paule Marshall and Kristin Hunter write about growing up in the city. Ms. Marshall's novel, *Brown Girl, Brownstones,* will introduce you to young Selina Boyce, who lives in Brooklyn, New York, with her Barbadian parents. You will follow her development into young womanhood as she comes to understand her own identity, sexuality, values, as well as learns to accept and respect the differences between her parents' aspirations as they confront poverty and racism in making America their new home. In Kristin Hunter's *The Soul Brothers and Sister Lou,* you will meet talented Louretta Hawkins whose love for her family and for music, especially popular songs, aid her in facing loneliness in the big city in which she lives. You will enjoy reading about her Black heritage. Also, you will like learning about how she becomes the lead singer in her group, "The Soul Brothers and Sister Lou." Most certainly, you will appreciate her unselfish sharing with her family of the money she receives as a successful pop singer.

These recommended readings are designed to peak your interest in the many books by Black women writers. Your school library, community library, and local bookstores are excellent resources to nurture your love for and appreciation of works by writers who speak both to and about you.

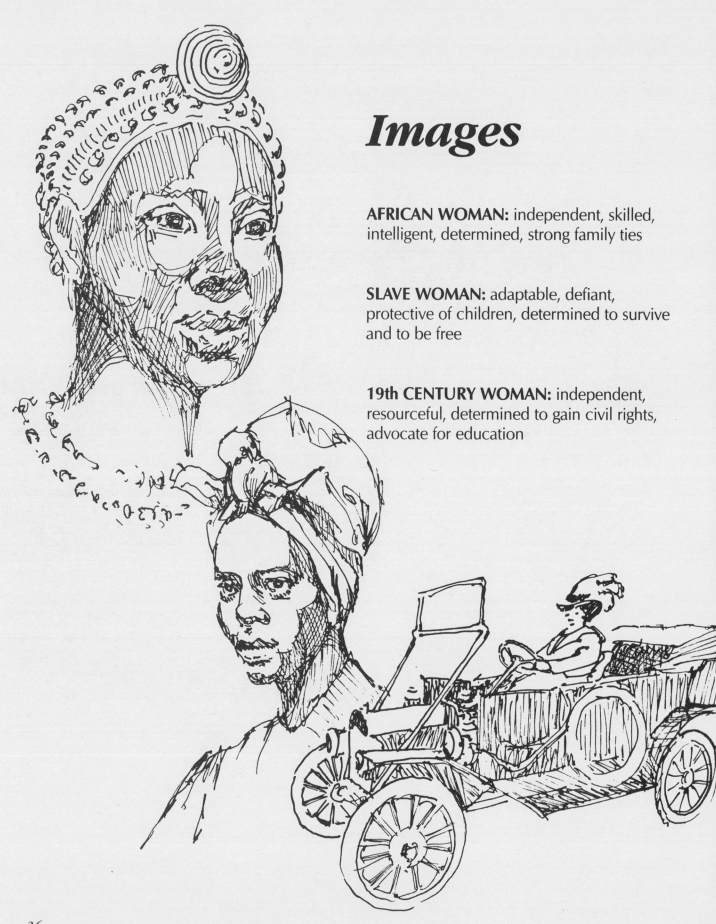

Images

AFRICAN WOMAN: independent, skilled, intelligent, determined, strong family ties

SLAVE WOMAN: adaptable, defiant, protective of children, determined to survive and to be free

19th CENTURY WOMAN: independent, resourceful, determined to gain civil rights, advocate for education

36

TODAY'S WOMAN: independent, intelligent, resourceful, determined to achieve

TOMORROW'S WOMAN: I am . . .

Chapter Two

HOW I GET ALONG WITH PEOPLE

As you continue your search for self, you will look more closely at your relationships with others. Who you are is determined to some extent by how you get along with other people. The motivation to achieve socially causes you to strive for satisfactory relationships with family members, friends, teachers, and other people with whom you have daily contact.

You try to live up to the expectations of other people, especially those close to you, in order to receive approval and respect from them. For example, when you work hard and get good grades, you please your family. You also benefit in several ways. In addition to establishing a good school record, you gain a sense of pride and confidence in your ability to achieve. In essence, your efforts to please others can lead to personal satisfaction.

Sometimes your desire to please others can cause you to violate your values and to behave in ways that lower your feelings of self-worth. For example, a relationship with a person who calls you names constantly or hurts you physically will cause you to like yourself less and less. Gradually, your lowered self-esteem will make you begin to believe that you deserve such treatment. You may even begin to make excuses for the other person's behavior. In this kind of relationship, you gain neither personal satisfaction nor the respect of the other person.

It is not necessary to sacrifice your pride and self-respect to try to win approval and recognition from other people. Rely on your own values and sense of personal power to guide you in relationships with family members, peers, and others.

During your search for self, you will learn more about other people. You will discover differences and similarities between them and you—in how you act, how you talk, how you think, and how you feel about things. As you know, individual differences exist even among people who grow up in the same family. Sometimes people are alike in many ways, even though they grew up in families and cultural environments that were quite different. Your relationships with other people are often made more interesting and exciting because you and they do not think and act the same way.

Being Different Does Not Have to Make a Difference

The black-eyed Susan is different from the carnation; neither is better than the other. It is all right for flowers to be different. Likewise, people, too, are different. People who are different from you should not be considered better than you. On the other hand, you should not feel that people are not as good as you are simply because they are different. As is true of flowers, every person is special and unique.

Go back and look at your family tree on page 20. Think about the people whom you chose to include. Why are they important to you? How do you get along with them? How would you like to change them?

Write about what you expect from the people who are close to you. Select the person who has the most influence over your behavior and decisions and complete:

•*I wish* _____

would _____

_____

_____

•*A true friend is somebody who* _____

_____

_____

_____

•*I consider* _____ *a true friend because*

_____

_____

_____

_____

•*I like boys who* _____

_____

_____

_____

You have just written about people who are important in your life. As you were thinking and writing, you probably made some interesting discoveries and learned that some of your expectations are selfish or unrealistic. Perhaps you expect the people close to you to give in to your wishes, or maybe you realized that you want more direction, support, or respect from them. No doubt, you have discovered that your attitudes and feelings toward others influence how you feel about yourself.

Sometimes your feelings about yourself are influenced by people you know only from a distance. Still you may compare yourself with them and decide that you would or would not like to be like them. Think about women you have observed and compare yourself with two of them.

Write a description of a woman you admire and compare yourself to her.

_____

_____

_____

_____

_____

_____

_____

_____

_____

_____

Write a description of a woman you dislike and compare yourself to her.

_____

_____

_____

_____

_____

_____

_____

_____

_____

_____

How Do You Communicate?

Before you started school, you could communicate. You were able to talk and express ideas clearly enough for others to understand and respond to you. As a small child, you learned a version of English that was used by family members and people close to you. When you went to school, you began to study English in order to learn more about the various ways the language can be used in writing and speaking.

You have probably discovered that you speak one way when talking with a close friend and another way when talking with a teacher or the school principal. You are able to communicate with people in various situations because of your awareness of the different ways English may be spoken. In other words, you know that you must use language that is appropriate for the situation. Just as you choose the clothing that you wear, you must also choose the language that you use.

When you communicate, you use actions as well as words. For example, you use facial expressions, posture, and hand movements. The words and actions that you use are called communication symbols. These symbols represent ideas that you want to express to another person. When you want to express yourself—send a message—you put together various combinations of symbols. Your choice of symbols depends on the person you are talking to and the social situation you are in at the time. You and the person you are talking to have to agree on the meaning of the symbols in order for your message to be understood.

How Do You Learn What the Symbols Mean?

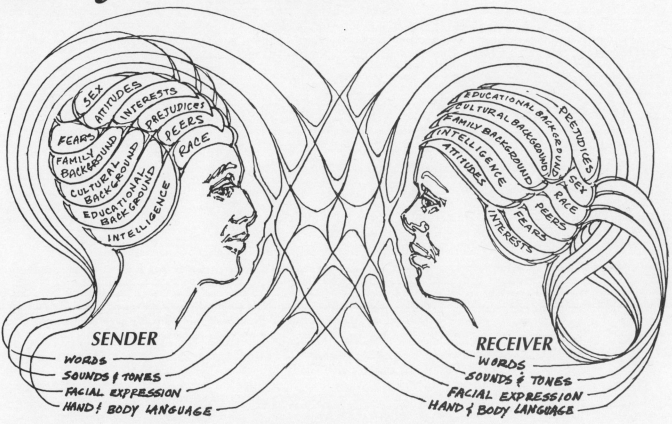

The illustration above shows you what happens when two people communicate with each other. The figures in the illustration represent you (sender) and the person you are talking to (receiver). The words woven into the hair of the sender and the receiver represent cultural influences that determine how people think and communicate. Ideas flow back and forth between the sender and the receiver by means of symbols: words, facial expressions, voice sounds and tones, hand movements, and body language.

As you were growing up, you learned to communicate through trial and error. You observed how family members used words, facial expressions, and body language in their conversations with one another. Then you imitated their behavior. By imitating others, you learned to use various communication symbols to express yourself. Through practice you learned to express your ideas well enough to be understood by other people and to have them respond to you.

45

What Happens When You Communicate?

When you talk to a person whose background is like yours, you both use similar words and expressions. Generally, you understand each other even though you may not agree. The important thing is that you understand each other.

When you and the other person do not have similar backgrounds, it may be difficult to communicate because the words and expressions that are used may not mean the same thing to both of you. Thus, the messages and responses that the two of you send back and forth may not be fully understood.

Sometimes you have to communicate with people whom you do not like in order to get information or assistance. Even though you may not like a person, you should not let that prevent you from trying to communicate in order to get what you need.

Think about the people with whom it is easy for you to communicate. Write about your experiences with some of these people.

•People I can talk with easily and why:

#1 _____

_____

_____

#2 _____

_____

_____

#3 _____

_____

_____

Think about the people with whom it is difficult for you to communicate. Write about your experiences with some of these people.

•People I can't talk with easily and why:

#1 _____

_____

_____

#2 _____

_____

_____

#3 _____

_____

_____

Review what you have just written. What makes it difficult for you to talk with these people? Is it because they disagree with you, or is it because they misunderstand you? Although the two are sometimes related, there is a difference between being misunderstood and having someone disagree with you.

Misunderstanding may occur because two people have different backgrounds and, therefore, use words and expressions that are not familiar to both of them. Sometimes people give different meanings to the same words or expressions. Misunderstanding may also occur because people are not willing to be honest with one another; that is, they do not say what they really mean. Disagreement may occur because people have different opinions about something. It is possible for a person to understand you and still disagree with you.

Remember: The goal in communication is to send and receive clear messages.

Think about a situation in which you were misunderstood by another person.
Write about what happened and why you were misunderstood.

_____

_____

_____

_____

•What did you learn from this experience? _____

_____

_____

_____

_____

•How could you have avoided being misunderstood? _____

_____

_____

_____

_____

Think about a situation in which you and another person disagreed about
something even though you understood one another clearly. What
happened? Why did you disagree?

•What did you learn from this experience? _____

_____

_____

_____

•What will you do differently next time? _____

_____

_____

_____

_____

48

Nonverbal Ways to Send a Message

   You have just finished thinking and writing about what happens sometimes when you talk with other people. As you were looking back at situations in which you were misunderstood, perhaps you realized that it was not something that you said. Maybe it was the way you looked or the way you acted that caused you to be misunderstood. More than you realize, practically every movement that you make sends a nonverbal message—a message without words. There are many nonverbal ways to send a message.

PHYSICAL APPEARANCE
How you look to people:
•choice of clothing
•hairstyle
•use of makeup

FACIAL EXPRESSION
What people see when they look in your face:
•frown
•smile
•smirk
•pout

HAND MOVEMENTS

How you use your hands when you talk with people:
- handshake
- clenched fist
- clapping
- nail biting
- pinching
- pointing
- pounding on table
- snapping fingers
- stroking
- wringing
- thumb up or down

EYE CONTACT

How you look at people:
- avoid eye contact
- direct eye contact
- glance
- raised eyebrows
- stare
- wink

USE OF SPACE

How close or how far you get when talking with people:
- face to face
- arms length
- several feet away

USE OF SOUND

How you use your voice:
- groan
- cough
- laugh
- moan
- mumble
- pause
- shout
- sigh
- silence
- whine
- whistle
- yawn

POSTURE/MOVEMENTS

How you sit, stand, walk:
- arms folded
- hands in pockets
- hands on hips
- pacing back and forth
- slouching
- squirming
- standing erect
- trembling

Language Behavior

The words and actions that you use to communicate may be referred to as language behavior. You have learned that in addition to using words, there are many other ways that you can send a message. You can put together a certain combination of words and actions so that your language behavior may be considered assertive, passive, or aggressive. The choices that you make are influenced by your self-concept and self-esteem as well as by the situations in which you have to communicate.

Your choice of language behavior is similar to your choice of clothing. Both make an impression and tell other people something about who you are.

WHAT YOUR LANGUAGE BEHAVIOR SAYS ABOUT YOU:

MEET IMA SERTIVE:

"I'll talk it over with you. Then I'll make up my mind."

ASSERTIVE:
She is self-confident, honest and direct; nevertheless, she is respectful of the opinions of others. She is willing to make her own decisions and assume responsibility for her own behavior.

PASSIVE:

She is willing to give in to others' demands. She is not honest about her true feelings, yet she becomes resentful when her ideas are ignored.

MEET IMA DOORMAT:

"All right, have it your way. I don't care."

MEET IMA BULLY:

"You can't tell me what to do. I'll do as I please."

AGGRESSIVE:

She is very direct, even hostile. She is not concerned about the feelings of others and thinks her own ideas are superior.

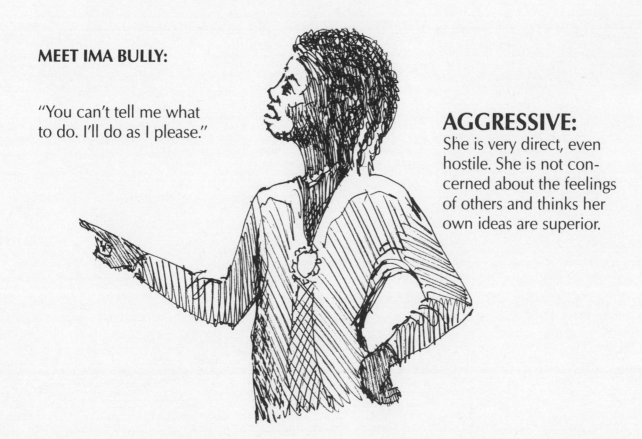

For each of the following situations, give assertive, passive, and aggressive responses. Then indicate which response would be most typical for you and why.

SITUATION #1:

Your friend, Ann, invites you and your cousin, Rita, to her birthday party. You and Rita decide to put your money together to purchase a gift. When you arrive at the party, Rita happens to be carrying the gift; she hands it to Ann. Later, when Ann opens the gift and sees the beautiful yellow blouse, she turns to Rita and says, "Oh, thank you, Rita; this is just what I wanted!" Rita says nothing.

•*The responses I could give in this situation:*

•*Assertive:* _____

_____

_____

_____

_____

•*Passive:* _____

_____

_____

_____

_____

•*Aggressive:* _____

_____

_____

_____

_____

•*The response most typical for me:* _____

•*Why?* _____

_____

_____

_____

SITUATION #2:

   You and your two sisters, ages 11 and 12, are expected to assist with household chores. Washing dishes is supposed to be shared so that each of you has two nights a week; your mother washes them on Sunday. It is not working out because your sisters fool around until it is close to their bedtime. Then they have to hurry and finish their homework so that they can get to bed. You end up washing dishes four or five times a week because you are the oldest and you are allowed to stay up until eleven o'clock. When you complain to your mother, she responds, "Oh, give them a break; they are still babies and need their rest."

•*The responses I could give in this situation:*

   •*Assertive:* _____
   _____
   _____
   _____
   _____
   _____

   •*Passive:* _____
   _____
   _____
   _____
   _____
   _____

   •*Aggressive:* _____
   _____
   _____
   _____
   _____
   _____

   •*The response most typical for me:* _____
   •*Why?* _____
   _____
   _____
   _____

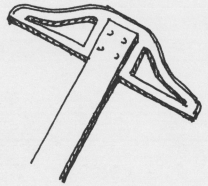

SITUATION #3:

Since elementary school you have been looking forward to going to college to study to become an engineer. You have taken a science class and have completed Pre-algebra and Algebra 1. You enjoyed the classes and made B's in all of them. Next semester is the beginning of your sophomore year. You need to decide which classes you should take so that you'll be able to apply for college when the time comes. You go in to get help from your counselor, who is surprised when you explain what your plans are. In fact, the counselor laughs and then asks, "Why do you want to take all that hard stuff? Why don't you make it light on yourself and take art and typing?"

•*The responses I could give in this situation:*

   •*Assertive:* _____

   _____

   _____

   _____

   _____

   •*Passive:* _____

   _____

   _____

   _____

   _____

   •*Aggressive:* _____

   _____

   _____

   _____

   _____

   •*The response most typical for me:* _____

   •*Why?* _____

   _____

   _____

   _____

SITUATION #4:

You and some friends are sitting in the park on Sunday afternoon talking and eating a picnic lunch. After talking about clothes, school, and the latest gossip, you get around to boyfriends and sex. Different girls tell a few jokes about personal escapades and exciting times; then somebody starts talking about "going all the way." According to what is said, everybody has had some experience except you. Suddenly, all eyes are on you and they begin to tease you about being a square, suggesting that you have to prove your love to hold a boyfriend. In fact, one of the girls admits proudly, "If you don't give in pretty soon, you're going to lose your boyfriend. He has his eyes on me and I'm going to take him up on it."

•*The responses I could give in this situation:*

    •*Assertive:* _____

_____

_____

_____

_____

    •*Passive:* _____

_____

_____

_____

_____

_____

    •*Aggressive:* _____

_____

_____

_____

_____

    •*The response most typical for me:* _____

    •*Why?* _____

_____

_____

_____

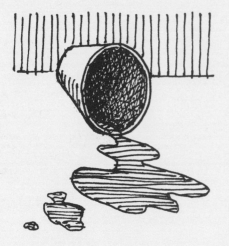

SITUATION #5:

You and Tyrone, a popular football player, met during the summer and have been dating each other ever since. You like him a lot, despite his violent temper. Twice he slapped you; both times he apologized and asked you to forgive him. You accepted his apologies and made him promise not to be so mean to you. You and Tyrone are together at the homecoming dance. He leaves you sitting alone while he goes to get punch and sandwiches for both of you. When he returns, you are chatting with Ricky, the quarterback. Immediately, Tyrone tosses the food and drinks on the floor and snatches you out of the chair. Then he starts shaking you and says angrily, "I'm gone two minutes and already you're flirting with some other guy. If I catch you talking to anybody else, I'm going to slap your face."

•*The responses I could give in this situation:*

    •*Assertive:* _____

_____

_____

_____

_____

    •*Passive:* _____

_____

_____

_____

_____

    •*Aggressive:* _____

_____

_____

_____

_____

    •*The response most typical for me:* _____

    •*Why?* _____

_____

_____

_____

WHAT DID YOU LEARN ABOUT YOUR LANGUAGE BEHAVIOR?

Indicate below your most typical response to each of the situations. Place a check in the appropriate column.

THE MOST TYPICAL RESPONSE FOR ME:			
SITUATION	ASSERTIVE	PASSIVE	AGGRESSIVE
#1			
#2			
#3			
#4			
#5			

Write a brief description of your language behavior.

_____

_____

_____

_____

_____

_____

What would you like to change?

_____

_____

_____

_____

_____

_____

Images: ASSERTIVE WOMEN

ROSAMOND BOLDEN
MANAGER

I am responsible for the management, maintenance, and operation of fifty-two state-owned buildings. My job title is Chief, Office of Buildings and Grounds, Department of General Services. Working under my management are 1,200 employees classified as stationary engineers, electricians, carpenters, painters, plumbers, janitors, groundskeepers, and clericals. I have held this position for ten years.

I began my career in state civil service as a Department of Employment representative trainee. My observation of the opportunities available in the workplace encouraged me to advance to employment counselor. I continued to take promotional civil service examinations and to obtain job assignments that advanced my career. Eventually, I attained a career executive assignment at the third level, my present position. To establish credibility in my occupation with my peers, I founded the Sacramento Chapter of Building Owners and Managers Association. Its purpose is to communicate the needs of the office building industry in Sacramento.

My college training was completed at the University of California, Berkeley. During my undergraduate years, I was often the only Black student in my classes. Nevertheless, I was successful in earning my Bachelor of Science degree in dietetics. In order to improve my skills and advance my career, I returned to the university and completed work for my master's degree in educational counseling psychology.

In high school I took college prep courses and maintained a position on the honor roll. Sometimes I was the only Black student in my college prep classes. I was shy, but I wanted to belong. Therefore, I was very observant and curious as well as active in school clubs.

Often now I am the only Black or the only female in my work setting. However, I am no longer shy. I am aggressively pursuing my career.

The office building is the **workplace** of this century. There are numerous career options available in this workplace. You can become a real estate agent, leasing officer, maintenance worker and, of course, a building manager. Each of these jobs requires skills and preparation that must begin while you are in high school.

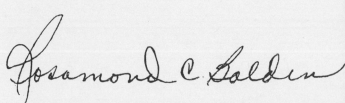

60

ALICE A. LYTLE
MUNICIPAL COURT JUDGE

After being appointed by the governor of California, I assumed my duties as a judge, Sacramento Municipal Court, in 1983. On a typical day, I preside over a number of different kinds of cases: misdemeanor trials, felony preliminary hearings, and court trials involving $25,000 or less.

In order to be a judge, you have to earn a college degree, graduate from law school, and practice law for at least five years. You must be intelligent, know the law, and have good character. In addition, you must be able to listen to people with an open mind and give them fair treatment.

I completed my legal training at Hastings College of Law in San Francisco and graduated with a Juris Doctor degree. I am a judge because friends and associates insisted that I should be. It turned out to be a good decision because not only am I a good judge, but I also thoroughly enjoy my work.

I was born into a very poor family and was only able to attend college because the city in which I lived had a free university system. My family was very supportive of my efforts to pursue my goals. I had to overcome many barriers; nevertheless, I was successful in earning a Bachelor of Arts degree in physiology and public health from Hunter College, New York City.

I do not remember much about high school because I did not enjoy it. In spite of the fact that I did not enjoy my high school experience, I did well in my studies.

During my law school career, I held various part-time positions with attorneys in the San Francisco Bay Area. After graduation but before I was licensed as a practicing attorney, I worked with the Public Defender's Office as a legal assistant. I participated in prison interviews with staff attorneys and assisted them during courtroom procedures.

It is difficult for young Black women to establish a career in law. You should not let difficulties or barriers stop you if your goal is a career in law. Your chances for success are greatly increased if you work hard and do your best.

Chapter Three

The world of work is not someplace "out there." It is where you are right now. Work is an integral part of your total life.

MY PLACE IN THE WORLD OF WORK

Have you ever given any thought to the meaning of work? Perhaps you think of work as "something hard that adults do to make money." Or maybe you think of work as "dull, boring chores that you have to perform at home." Perhaps you really do not think about work very much because "that's something you'll do sometime in the future."

In many ways you are already very much involved in the world of work. Let's look at the meaning of work to see how it includes you and what you do everyday.

WORK IS:

• An activity that contributes to self-esteem by providing opportunities to develop competence in dealing with ideas, things, and people.

• An activity that provides opportunities to meet and interact with other people.

• An activity that produces something of value for other people.

• An activity that contributes to self-sufficiency.

Compare some of your daily activities at school, at home, and in your community with those used to define work. Now list some of the things that you do that you consider work.

CONTRIBUTES TO SELF-ESTEEM

Example: serve as class president

_____

_____

_____

_____

PROVIDES OPPORTUNITIES TO MEET PEOPLE

Example: sing in church choir

_____

_____

_____

_____

PRODUCES SOMETHING OF VALUE

Example: make costume jewelry

_____

_____

_____

_____

CONTRIBUTES TO SELF-SUFFICIENCY

Example: make my own clothes

_____

_____

_____

_____

As you can see, you already have a place in the world of work.

Write your definition of work.

_____

_____

_____

_____

_____

Skills for the Information and Service Society

THINKING   PROBLEM SOLVING   CREATING   LEARNING

WHAT WILL BE HAPPENING IN THE WORLD OF WORK?

•People will be producing and distributing information.

•Demands will be changing constantly. Workers will have to be retrained numerous times in order to keep up with the demands for new ideas and information.

•Consumers will be demanding more services. There will be many opportunities for people to be creative and to start their own businesses in order to meet consumer demands.

•Workers will need to know:

•**HOW TO COMMUNICATE -** the ability to express ideas clearly in written and verbal forms.

•**HOW TO CREATE -** ability to use individual ideas to develop new products and services.

•**HOW TO LEARN -** ability to change and adapt; willingness to learn new ways of doing things.

•**HOW TO SOLVE PROBLEMS -** ability to identify problems, examine facts, and reach logical conclusions.

•**HOW TO THINK -** ability to put facts together and draw conclusions.

•**HOW TO USE COMPUTERS -** ability to gather and share information quickly and accurately through the use of data and word processors.

Will there be a place for you in the world of work?

From Schoolwork to Paid Employment

In the future, the world of work will provide many opportunities for people to operate their own businesses. It is possible that someday you could be in a position to hire people to work for you. What kind of workers would you want in your company?

List habits and attitudes that you would expect your employees to have:

_____

_____

_____

_____

_____

_____

_____

_____

What Kind of Worker Are You?

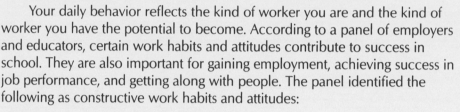

Your daily behavior reflects the kind of worker you are and the kind of worker you have the potential to become. According to a panel of employers and educators, certain work habits and attitudes contribute to success in school. They are also important for gaining employment, achieving success in job performance, and getting along with people. The panel identified the following as constructive work habits and attitudes:

- Realistic positive attitude toward self
- Positive attitude toward work
- Pride in accomplishment
- Willingness to learn
- Dependable and able to follow through on a task
- Regular and punctual attendance
- Ability to set goals and allow time to achieve them
- Willingness to follow rules
- An understanding of the need for supervision
- Ability to accept responsibility
- Appropriate dress and grooming
- Freedom from substance abuse
- Appropriate personal hygiene

Use the list of work habits above to evaluate your own work habits and attitudes. List each statement under one of the following headings.

MY SATISFACTORY WORK HABITS AND ATTITUDES	WORK HABITS AND ATTITUDES I NEED TO IMPROVE
_____	_____
_____	_____
_____	_____
_____	_____
_____	_____
_____	_____

NOTE: The work habits and attitudes listed were adapted from those the panel identified. See *High Schools and the Changing Workplace: An Employer's View* (Washington, D.C.: National Academy Press, 1984) 27.

THE PERFORMANCE EVALUATION

Periodically, your teachers evaluate your performance as a student by means of a grading system. Grades are used to make such decisions as to whether or not you pass or fail a course, move on to the next academic level, or graduate from high school. Employers will also evaluate your job performance from time to time to determine whether you should be allowed to remain on the job or whether you deserve a raise or promotion. The work habits and attitudes that you have just written about are examples of the criteria that employers use to evaluate their employees. The following is an example of an evaluation sheet.

PERFORMANCE EVALUATION

			From: To:
Last Name	First Name	Initial	Period Covered by Report

Classification   Department

Please place an "X" in the appropriate box, and in the "Comments." section, show how the factor is related to this particular job; give specific reasons and/or examples for assigning the rating checked.

Column headers (diagonal): Unacceptable, Need to Improve, Average, Above Average, Outstanding

WORK HABITS: Organization of work; care of equipment; safety; punctuality; attendance
COMMENTS:

ATTITUDE: Enthusiasm for the work; willingness to conform to job requirements and to accept suggestions for work improvement
COMMENTS:

QUALITY OF WORK: Accuracy; completeness; neatness
COMMENTS:

QUANTITY OF WORK: Amount of acceptable work turned out
COMMENTS:

RELATIONSHIPS WITH PEOPLE: Ability to get along with others; effectiveness in dealing with the public
COMMENTS:

INITIATIVE: Self-reliance; resourcefulness; willingness and ability to accept and carry out responsibility
COMMENTS:

DEPENDABILITY: Reliability; ability to meet deadlines without close supervision
COMMENTS:

PERSONAL FITNESS: Emotional stability; physical condition; appearance; habits
COMMENTS:

Discussed report with employee   ___ Yes ___ No

Signature of Rater_____ Title _____ Date _____

Signature of Employee_____ Date _____

My Work Values — What I Would Look for in a Job

As you read the list of work values below, think about how important each work value is to you. List the statements that tell what you would definitely expect on a job.

WORK VALUES

- Have challenges.
- Do a variety of things.
- Work with people I like.
- Be my own boss.
- Have a set routine.
- Work with my mind.
- Have a chance for promotion.
- Work with my hands.
- Meet many new people.
- Be told what to do.
- Work as part of a team.
- Invent or design things.
- Develop new ideas.
- Supervise other people.
- Receive recognition for my work.
- Have opportunity to learn new skills.

- Be well paid.
- Help others.
- Do exciting things.
- Wear casual clothing.
- Work indoors.
- Do outdoor work.
- Wear business clothes.
- Work alone most of the time.
- Handle heavy responsibility.
- Set my own hours.
- Do physical work.
- Influence other people.
- Have people look up to me.
- Make decisions on my own.
- Work in pleasant surroundings.
- Receive personal satisfaction.

WORK VALUES IMPORTANT TO ME

_____

_____

_____

_____

_____

_____

_____

_____

_____

_____

_____

_____

_____

_____

_____

_____

_____

Transition to Paid Employment—

EMPLOYEE, ENTREPRENEUR, OR BOTH

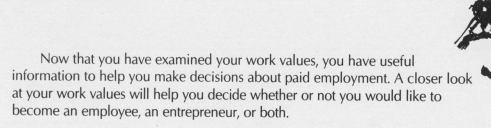

Now that you have examined your work values, you have useful information to help you make decisions about paid employment. A closer look at your work values will help you decide whether or not you would like to become an employee, an entrepreneur, or both.

BECOMING AN EMPLOYEE

Most of the people in the workforce are employees: They work for someone else in exchange for a salary and other forms of compensation.

You have already learned the meaning of work and have written your own definition. In addition, you have assessed your own work habits. Becoming an employee also requires a **work attitude—an awareness of some basic information and practices that are essential in the world of work.**

ELEMENTS OF A WORK ATTITUDE
ADAPTABILITY TO WORK ENVIRONMENT

- Conform to standards for behavior.
- Demonstrate respect for authority.
- Get along with coworkers even if I do not like them.
- Dress in suitable attire.
- Reflect a positive image of the company.
- Learn and use appropriate language.

KNOWLEDGE OF VOCABULARY AND PRACTICES RELATED TO THE WORLD OF WORK.

Contract - an agreement between two or more persons to do something.

Fringe benefits - extras, such as sick leave and vacation pay, that an employer provides for workers.

Health insurance - a means of making sure that a worker receives money to pay doctors' bills and medical expenses.

Income tax - money a worker pays to the government based on the amount of earnings and number of dependents.

Workers' Compensation - payment a worker receives because of illness or injury caused by the job.

Minimum wage - the lowest wage, determined by law or contract, that an employer is allowed to pay a worker.

Pension - payment from a special fund that a person receives after retirement.

Social Security tax - money a worker pays into a retirement fund held by the federal government.

Unemployment insurance - temporary payment a worker receives if she loses her job and is unable to find another.

Labor union - a group of workers joined together to promote favorable working conditions.

BECOMING AN ENTREPRENEUR

An entrepreneur is a person who finds a need for a service or product and then develops a business to meet that need. According to one successful entrepreneur, there are three major components of a business plan:

•Your business goal;
•A marketing and sales strategy to determine who your customers are and how to make them buy your products or services; and
•A financial plan that includes how much money it will take to start and maintain your business.

Women are becoming entrepreneurs at a faster rate than men. Perhaps this is because they are more accustomed than men to meeting demands for personal and educational services. Shopping, cooking, babysitting, sewing, styling hair, writing, and planning activities are all skills that can be turned into a service for others by following the plan outlined above. These skills can be used in several business areas that are projected for growth into the twenty-first century:

•All types of personal services
•Care of the elderly
•More efficient fast food service
•Video services
•Health care products and services
•Specialty shops
•Computerized services

The emerging service economy is expected to continue to open opportunities for women who are willing to risk starting businesses of their own. If you decided that you wanted to turn your skills into a money-making enterprise, you could obtain information from business teachers as well as librarians and from women who are already operating their own businesses.

Successful women entrepreneurs are independent, self-confident, and self-directed. They also know how to manage people and money. Because so much depends on them, they have to be action-oriented and capable of making sound decisions. There are rewards to be gained from the risk-taking and hard work. In addition to the financial gain, women entrepreneurs have the assurance that whatever they achieve is due largely to their own creativity, skills, and intelligence. Aside from the personal rewards, they make an important contribution to society by providing jobs for others.

WOULD YOU LIKE TO:
•Have challenges?
•Handle heavy responsibility and constant planning?
•Use your skills to earn money for yourself?
•Make decisions on your own?
•Be your own boss?

Perhaps you have the potential to become an entrepreneur.

> *"Starting a business is easy, but surviving in business is the name of the game."*
>
> — **Dolores Ratcliffe, President, Association of Black Women Entrepreneurs, Los Angeles**

The Nontraditional World of Work

Have you ever noticed that most of the nurses that you see are women and most of the carpenters are men? You probably grew up thinking that it was **just supposed to be that way**. It is true that beliefs and customs handed down from one generation to the next have made it seem natural for the workforce to be divided between "women's jobs" and "men's jobs." Indeed, it has been traditional for women to be secretaries and nurses and for men to be plumbers and carpenters.

In general, jobs considered only for women have offered low pay and few opportunities for advancement. This practice was based on the assumption that because their husbands could take care of them, women who worked would do so for only a short time. Then they would leave the job market and go home to take care of their families. Therefore, there was no need to pay them high salaries.

Through the years such employment practices have placed Black women at a disadvantage. Traditionally, they have worked even though they had husbands and children. Limited job opportunities forced many of them to work as service workers, such as cooks and housekeepers. They accepted these jobs that offered low pay and poor working conditions because their families needed the income in order to survive.

As you explore career options, it is important to consider nontraditional employment from the perspective of your cultural heritage. In other words, movement from service jobs to clerical and health-related jobs is nontraditional for many Black women. Such movement is an effective means of establishing a base for job mobility. An expression from your cultural folklore says it well: "If you get one job, you can get another."

According to the U.S. Department of Labor, since 1970 there has been a decline in the number of Black women in household work and an increase in the number employed in blue-collar occupations, such as bus driver, delivery person, and truck driver. There has also been an increase in the number of Black women employed in many professional and technical jobs. Though the progress has been limited, more Black women are now employed in sales, management and administration, and administrative support positions.

In summary, Black women have made inroads into the nontraditional world of work on more than one level. There is every reason to believe that these trends will continue, especially since more and more job opportunities are opening up for all women.

BLACK WOMEN IN THE EXPERIENCED CIVILIAN LABOR FORCE IN THE UNITED STATES, 1980*

Selected Occupations	Number Employed
Bus drivers	22,652
Carpenters, except apprentices	2,546
Child care workers, except private household	87,291
Computer operators	28,041
Computer programmers	7,934
Construction laborers	5,521
Cooks, except short order	153,457
Data-entry keyers	60,887
Electricians, except apprentices	1,712
Engineers	4,517
Financial records processing	102,247
Firefighting and fire prevention	333
General office clerks	181,672
Guards	23,252
Hairdressers and cosmetologists	33,623
Lawyers	4,272
Licensed practical nurses	75,698
Machine operators, assorted materials	170,054
Management related	86,524
Managers and administrators, salaried	76,687
Material moving equipment operators	10,642
Material recording, scheduling and distributing clerks	70,652
Mechanics and repairers	17,846
Painters, construction and maintenance	2,715
Physicians	3,245
Police and detectives	9,792
Postal clerks, except mail carriers	32,773
Precision production	90,164
Records processing occupations, except financial	105,984
Registered nurses	91,534
Sales representatives, finance and business services	25,907
Sales workers, retail and personal services	277,500
Secretaries	227,552
Social workers	61,547
Teachers, except postsecondary	288,876
Teachers, postsecondary	15,596
Truck drivers, heavy	6,235

*U.S. Department of Commerce, Bureau of Census, 1980 Census of Population/EEO Special File.

Images: ENTREPRENEURS

TIA HUNNICUTT
DOLL ARTIST AND MANUFACTURER

I live in San Francisco, and I am a full-time high school honor student carrying a heavy academic load. Homework consumes much of my time because I plan to attend college. Yet I still find time for my other love—doll making. I devote at least two hours a day to doll making. The ultimate satisfaction for me is making dolls that bring smiles to faces and joy to hearts.

I studied with three doll makers in order to develop my skills. I make over sixty different porcelain reproduction dolls as well as my own original cloth dolls. The porcelain dolls require the most production time since they must be researched according to period, culture, and ethnicity. Then each part must be cast in molds, cleaned, fired, and painted. If necessary, the dolls are then fired, painted, and refired. I design most of the clothes, and my staff sews them.

The initial barrier to becoming an entrepreneur is raising cash once you have researched your business and developed a feasible business plan. Fortunately, my family and friends donated $10,000 to get me started. Of course, additional funds are needed so that my business can develop and expand. To raise these funds, I work at another job during the summer. Family members, interested investors, and friends provide additional funds.

Marketing my products requires skill and creativity. My dolls are featured in five gift shops in California. I am developing a direct mail operation for out of state and international customers. I am continually looking for opportunities to reach new customers through retail store outlets and innovative marketing.

A good education is imperative whether a person is an entrepreneur or a laborer. Therefore, I work hard to get good grades so that I can rely on my education if my business sales diminish.

As a small business entrepreneur, I have struggled to succeed. My efforts have won me numerous honors and awards. I am especially proud that the San Francisco Chamber of Commerce recognized my achievements and, in 1986, named me "Minority Entrepreneur of the Future."

I firmly believe that struggle is the essence of life. It takes hard work, dedication, and sacrifice to be creative and to produce quality products for the buying public. The opportunity to succeed is worth the struggle.

Tia Hunnicutt

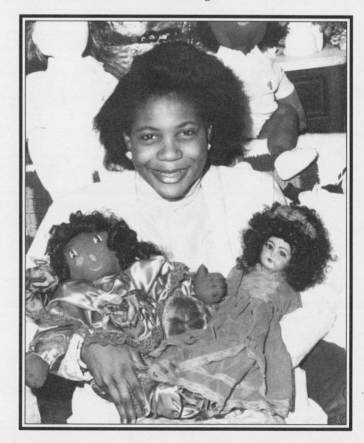

JOSEPHINE RICHARDSON
OWNER, SECURITY COMPANY

The company that I own is a highly specialized security service. It has provided guards and patrol personnel to a variety of public and private industries in northern California for seventeen years. As chief executive officer, I am responsible for up to 400 employees.

My business career began when I helped my husband operate a security escort service. After we divorced, I decided to open my own company. I enrolled in the Industrial College of the Armed Forces in Los Angeles so that I could acquire additional skills to operate my business efficiently. I received a two year certificate in international security and business management.

My company generates new and repeat business of over $2,000,000 annually and has been making a profit since it began in 1969. I have never borrowed a dime, and I have never gone to the government or to anyone for anything. I manage the company finances well and never overspend what the business receives. My management skills and achievements have won me respect from my peers. I was proud to receive a recognition award from the Bay Area Women Entrepreneurs.

Building a successful business has given me a great deal of personal satisfaction as well as financial security. Many times I have thought about retiring, but I can't imagine life without work. My goal is to make my company grow so that it earns over $10 million a year.

One of the things that satisfies me most is the opportunity to share my time and money with others.

Giving makes me feel better about myself. Each year I donate between $25,000 and $50,000 to charitable organizations. I serve on a number of community boards and sometimes attend up to four meetings a day. I do not mind doing volunteer work as long as my efforts have a positive impact on my community.

The cause that I feel most strongly about is America's youth. I have worked with teenagers for more than thirty-five years. I believe they need lots of direction to help them face today's challenges. As a role model, that is why it is so important for me to spend time talking to young people such as you. As you prepare for the future, I want you to remember that success is only obtained by the person who wants it.

Josephine Richardson

PART II

Your journey into the future has already begun. Your destination — where you will go — will depend upon your willingness to develop your potential and to set goals that you believe you can reach.

Where Am I Going?

Chapter Four

There aren't two worlds—education and work—one for youth, the other for maturity. There is one world—life.
                                    - Author Unknown

FROM LEARNING TO EARNING

You have discovered that school is a part of the real world, not a place to stop off on the way to becoming an adult. You have also learned that the world of work is the real world that you live in every day. You have already begun your career—your total life experience. In the school setting you learn how to achieve academically and how to get along with your peers. You also develop skills and acquire knowledge that can help you as you prepare for a satisfying career and life-style.

Science and Mathematics: Knowledge That Will Open Doors

There are many career options open to women and men who have studied science and mathematics. Technical occupations in the fast-growing health and medical services, in communications, and in the military service require the ability to work with electronic and mechanical equipment. Many jobs of the future will demand skills and experience that you can acquire in laboratory work related to your physics, chemistry, and biology classes.

> **You do not have to be a genius to study mathematics and science.**

IF YOU ARE . . .
- CURIOUS
- PERSISTENT
- INTELLIGENT
- LOGICAL

IF YOU LIKE TO . . .
- Create new ways to do things
- Discover what makes things work
- Find solutions to problems

THERE MAY BE A PLACE FOR YOU IN SCIENCE AND TECHNOLOGY

. . . as a chemist
. . . as an engineer
. . . as a biologist
. . . on a construction site
. . . as a food scientist
. . . as an x-ray technologist
. . . as a physical therapist
. . . as a medical technician
. . . in a classroom
. . . as a systems analyst

. . . as an electrician
. . . as an electronics technician
. . . as an accountant
. . . as a drafting technician
. . . as a physician
. . . as a physician's assistant
. . . in a hospital
. . . in an office
. . . in a laboratory
. . . as a math teacher

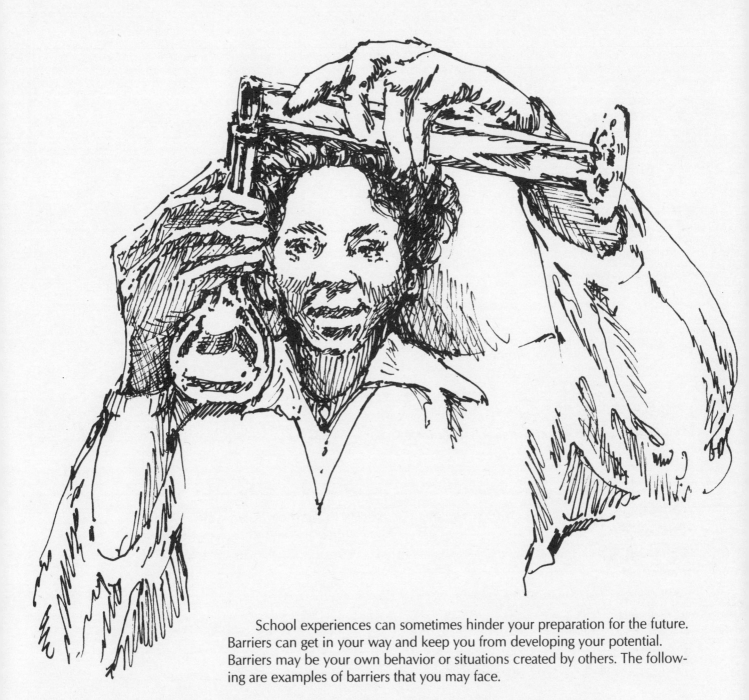

School experiences can sometimes hinder your preparation for the future. Barriers can get in your way and keep you from developing your potential. Barriers may be your own behavior or situations created by others. The following are examples of barriers that you may face.

For each barrier listed below, write a statement that tells one thing you would do to overcome it.

•*Follow the crowd so I can be popular.* _____

_____

_____

•*Don't try to do the work if I don't like the teacher.* _____

_____

_____

•*Fear criticism from friends if I get good grades.*_____

_____

_____

•*Receive unfair treatment because of my race.*_____

_____

_____

•*Feel grades don't matter.* _____

_____

_____

•*Show no interest in student government.*_____

_____

_____

•*Don't bother with extracurricular activities.*_____

_____

_____

•*Don't try to get help when I am having trouble with an assignment.*_____

_____

_____

•*Don't bother to ask questions in class.*_____

_____

_____

•*Don't try to get help from my counselor.*_____

_____

_____

•*Receive unfair treatment because I am a girl.*_____

_____

_____

•*Give too much time to extracurricular activities.* _____
_____
_____

•*Don't get enough help from my counselor.* _____
_____
_____

•*Avoid math and science classes because I think they are too hard.* _____
_____
_____

•*Tune out when classes are boring.* _____
_____
_____

•*Skip classes to be with my friends.* _____
_____
_____

•*Avoid foreign language classes because I think they are too hard.* _____
_____
_____

•*Don't feel school is related to anything.* _____
_____
_____

•*Put off doing my homework and let myself get behind.* _____
_____
_____

•*Other* _____
_____
_____

Developing Competencies: From Classroom to Job Market

When you enter the job market, you will probably expect to receive a good salary and benefits, have opportunities for promotions, and gain satisfaction from your work. According to a panel of employers and educators, jobs that will enable you to meet your expectations will require you to be competent in a number of areas. The panel has identified the following eight competency areas that are essential for almost every job except the least skilled:

1. COMMAND OF THE ENGLISH LANGUAGE
2. READING
3. WRITING
4. REASONING AND PROBLEM-SOLVING
5. COMPUTATION
6. SOCIAL STUDIES AND ECONOMICS
7. SCIENCE AND TECHNOLOGY
8. ORAL COMMUNICATION

Review the competency areas and record your plans for developing your skills:

#1 COMMAND OF THE ENGLISH LANGUAGE:

A functional command of standard English is the most basic skill of all.

MY PLAN FOR DEVELOPING SKILLS IN THIS AREA

COURSES COMPLETED	COURSES TAKING	COURSES TO TAKE	EXTRACURRICULAR ACTIVITIES

#2 READING:

Competent reading requires the ability to:

•Understand the purpose of written material.
•Note details and facts.
•Identify and summarize main and related ideas.
•Interpret charts, tables, and graphs.

MY PLAN FOR DEVELOPING SKILLS IN THIS AREA

COURSES COMPLETED	COURSES TAKING	COURSES TO TAKE	EXTRACURRICULAR ACTIVITIES

#3 WRITING:

Skillful writing requires the ability to:

•Gather information suitable for the topic.
•Organize information in a logical manner.
•Use complete sentences.
•Apply the rules for correct spelling, punctuation, and capitalization.
•Use reference books such as the dictionary.
•Write legibly.

MY PLAN FOR DEVELOPING SKILLS IN THIS AREA

COURSES COMPLETED	COURSES TAKING	COURSES TO TAKE	EXTRACURRICULAR ACTIVITIES

#4 REASONING AND PROBLEM-SOLVING:

A person with well-developed reasoning ability is able to:

•Identify problems.
•Consider and evaluate possible solutions.
•Make logical decisions.
•Separate fact from opinion.
•Adjust to unexpected situations.
•Decide how to complete work assignments.

MY PLAN FOR DEVELOPING SKILLS IN THIS AREA

COURSES COMPLETED	COURSES TAKING	COURSES TO TAKE	EXTRACURRICULAR ACTIVITIES

#5 COMPUTATION:

Precise computation requires the ability to:

•Add, subtract, multiply, and divide whole numbers, decimals,
 and fractions.
•Compute distance, weight, area, volume, and time.
•Determine the amount of money, time, and resources required to
 complete a task.
•Calculate simple interest.
•Compute costs and make change.
•Use information from charts, graphs, and tables to make
 calculations.
•Make estimates and judge their accuracy.

MY PLAN FOR DEVELOPING SKILLS IN THIS AREA

COURSES COMPLETED	COURSES TAKING	COURSES TO TAKE	EXTRACURRICULAR ACTIVITIES

#6 SOCIAL STUDIES AND ECONOMICS:

Adequate knowledge in these areas includes an understanding of:

- The history of American society.
- The political, economic, and social system of America and other nations.
- The fundamentals of economics, such as a basic understanding of the role of money.
- How employers and employees fit into the American economy.
- The structure and functions of local, state, and federal governments.
- Citizen rights and responsibilities.
- Civil rights and justice in a free society.

MY PLAN FOR DEVELOPING SKILLS IN THIS AREA

COURSES COMPLETED	COURSES TAKING	COURSES TO TAKE	EXTRACURRICULAR ACTIVITIES

#7 SCIENCE AND TECHNOLOGY:

Competence in science and technology requires the ability to:

• Apply the scientific method.
• Apply the basic principles of the physical, chemical, and biological
  sciences.
• Understand the basic functions of computers.

MY PLAN FOR DEVELOPING SKILLS IN THIS AREA

COURSES COMPLETED	COURSES TAKING	COURSES TO TAKE	EXTRACURRICULAR ACTIVITIES

#8 ORAL COMMUNICATION:

Competence in oral communication includes the ability to:

•Communicate in standard English.
•Understand and give instructions.
•Identify and summarize main and related ideas in discussions.
•Ask clear, specific questions.
•Participate effectively in discussions.

MY PLAN FOR DEVELOPING SKILLS IN THIS AREA

COURSES COMPLETED	COURSES TAKING	COURSES TO TAKE	EXTRACURRICULAR ACTIVITIES

NOTE: The competency areas and related skills are adapted from those identified by the panel of educators and employers. See *High Schools and the Changing Workplace: An Employer's View* (Washington, D.C.: National Academy Press, 1984) 20-27.

Journey to Futureville

You have just completed a demanding but very important assessment of your academic record. Now you are going to use that information as a guide to take a make-believe journey to Futureville.

The major stops along the way to Futureville are English Town, Social Studies City, Math Mesa, Foreign Language Land, Science Heights, Vocational Vista, Village of the Arts, and Elective Gardens.

Some of these places are familiar because you have visited them before. Based on your career plans, you may plan to visit several places later. You will probably choose to pass up some stops because they do not fit into your plans.

On your travel map circle the places that you have visited already. Place an *X* next to the places that you plan to visit. You will need to write in the names of places that are not on the map.

ALL ABOARD—ENJOY YOUR TRIP!

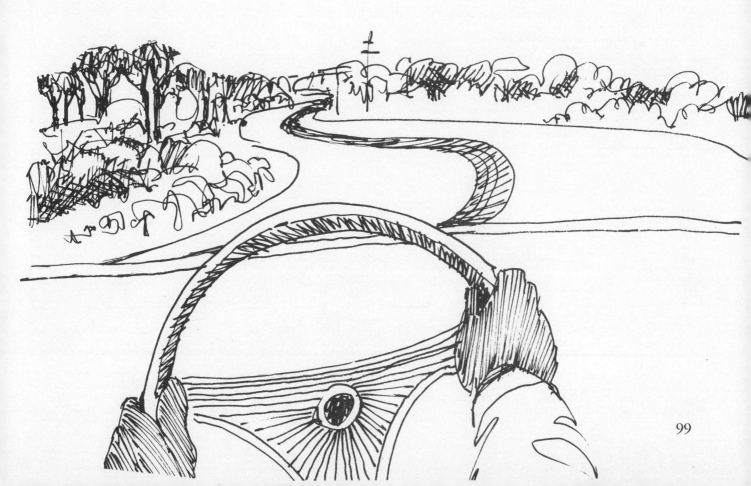

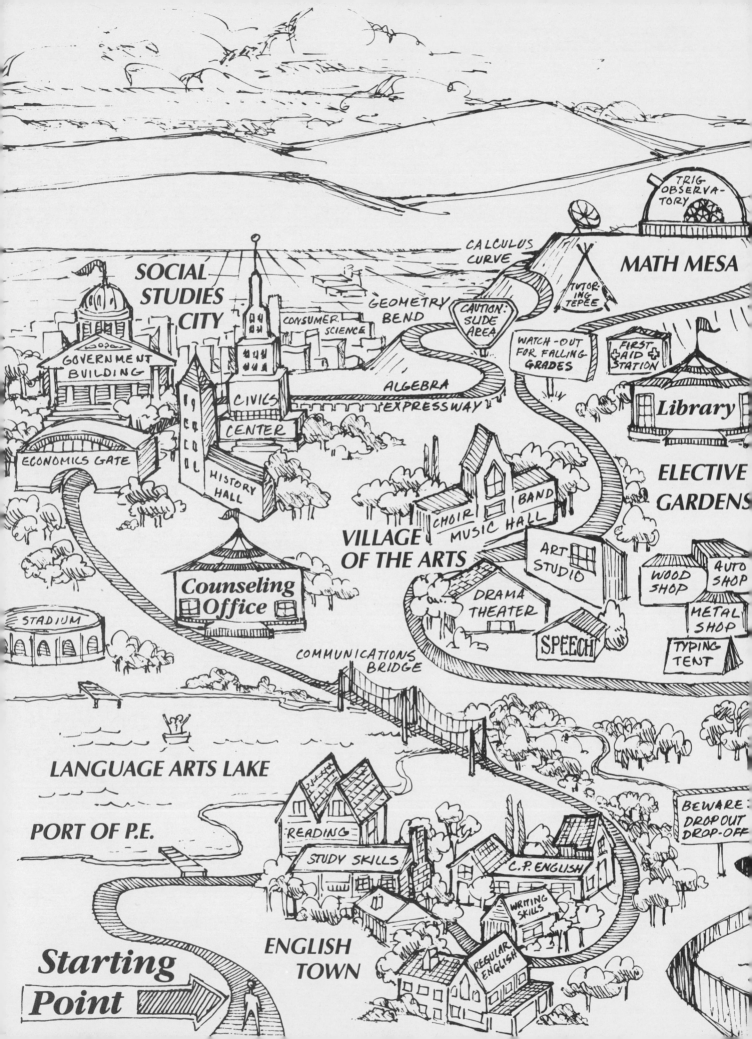

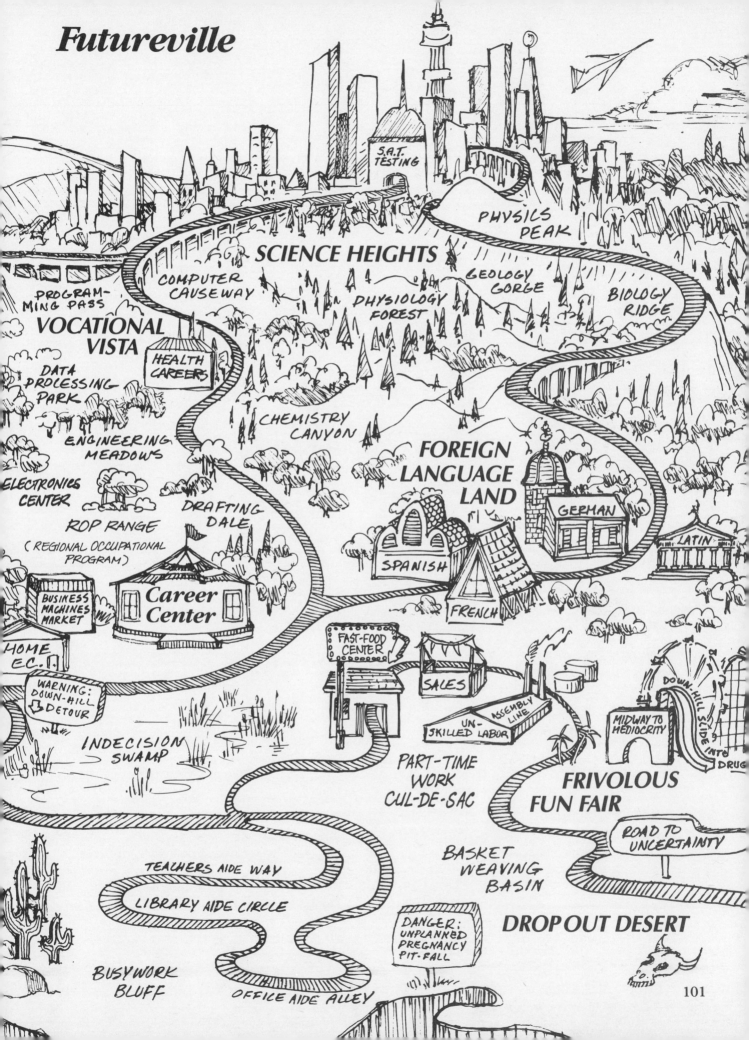

WELCOME BACK FROM FUTUREVILLE!!

You probably learned a lot about yourself during your journey. No matter what grade you are in, it should be clear to you that you have established a record. That record is going to affect the outcome of your future as a student and as an adult in the world of work. You must be sure that your record reflects your potential to learn and achieve.

If you are not satisfied with what you have learned about yourself and your academic record, then **you need to consider what you can do to change your behavior and maybe even your attitude**.

By the way, did you take advantage of those special free tours to the career center, the library, and the counseling center?

Make your school experiences work for you, not against you. Be assertive; take an active role in making decisions about your classes and activities. Don't just let things happen to you.

All of these resources are available to help you learn and develop your potential.

- teachers
- schoolmates
- career center
- counselor
- principal
- custodian
- food service
- bulletin boards
- library
- clerical staff
- school nurse
- vice principal

ASK QUESTIONS . . .
SEEK INFORMATION . . .
USE THE RESOURCES IN YOUR SCHOOL ENVIRONMENT.

Unless you call out, who will open the door?
                                    - African Proverb

PAMELA SPEARMAN
DESIGN ENGINEER

My position is that of design engineer at a refinery. My duties include designing and troubleshooting equipment that is used to produce gasoline, such as pumps, heat exchangers, and pressure vessels. I have also spent time recruiting engineers on college campuses.

When I was choosing a career, I wanted a job that would not require a lot of physical labor and would not require me to punch a clock. In addition, I wanted to make enough money to live comfortably. When I learned about engineering through the Mathematics, Engineering, and Science Achievement (MESA) program at my high school, I decided to become a chemical engineer because I liked chemistry.

To become an engineer, you need to take a lot of science and math in junior and senior high school. It is also necessary to obtain a Bachelor of Science degree in engineering from a four-year college. An alternative to obtaining a B.S. degree is to get a two-year degree (Associate of Science) from a community college or technical school, and then pursue a career as an engineering technician. The long-term career paths are different for engineers and technicians. Therefore, you should talk to people in the field before making your decision.

When I was in high school, my long-term plans were to go to college and get a job so that I could get out on my own and not have to depend on anyone for financial support. Two things were planted firmly in my mind: I would not have a baby until I completed my education and got married, and I would not do drugs.

If I were back in high school, I would learn how to study more efficiently. I would also have more confidence in myself and not worry so much about being popular.

I was used to getting good grades in high school without too much effort. The most difficult barrier I had to overcome in college was the temptation to give up when the courses got tough. When they did, I put my faith in God and pressed onward.

The future outlook is bright for Black women in technical fields. If you do not think you would like to become a chemical engineer, other branches of engineering you can consider are mechanical, civil, industrial, nuclear, and electrical. I encourage you to seriously consider a technical career and remember— you can do it.

Pamela Spearman

SCIENCE AND TECHNOLOGY

CAROLINE L. LEDBETTER
PHYSICIST

I am employed as a physicist with the Naval Weapons Station, Seal Beach, Corona Annex. I chose this occupation because it provides a variety of work experiences, financial security and stability, and opportunities for professional and personal growth. An average day at work consists of preparing for management correspondence on my assigned projects, attending meetings, and providing technical assistance to personnel at Navy Calibration on matters pertaining to electronic equipment.

To prepare myself for a professional career, I attended Clark College in Atlanta, Georgia, where I received a Bachelor of Arts degree in physics. While in college, I spent my summers working as an intern at various companies. Through this work experience, I learned how to apply my academic training to jobs that required a background in physics.

I grew up in Bennettsville, a rural manufacturing town in South Carolina. The likelihood of getting out and becoming successful was not good. My mother instilled in me the belief that I could do or be anything I desired; as a result, I longed to do that which I was told I was not able to do. My father died when I was six years old. Watching my mother struggle to raise eight children alone convinced me that I wanted to do more than just get by. I decided that education was my ticket to success.

In high school most of the Black girls were encouraged to take general or vocational classes. I chose to enroll in college preparatory classes such as biology, chemistry, algebra, physics, trigonometry, and calculus.

I wanted to be a well-rounded person, so I got involved in school activities: student council, science club, and girls varsity basketball. Involvement in these activities taught me responsibility, teamwork, leadership skills, and how to get along with people.

I have been fortunate; personally, I have not faced any outward sexual or racial barriers. Nevertheless, I am aware that they are real and do still exist. To those who have faced barriers and have overcome them, I say, "Well done." To those who are now facing barriers or may face them in the future, I say, "Believe in yourself and your abilities; do not give up and have faith in God."

As we continue to move toward a more technologically advanced world, the future of Black women with degrees in physics looks very promising. There will be opportunities available for you in career fields such as education, research, medicine, electronics, and aerospace.

Caroline L. Ledbetter

Chapter Five

WHAT ARE MY CAREER OPTIONS?

Whether you get married or not, you can expect to be in the workforce about forty years; you can also expect to change jobs several times.

Planning Your Career/Life-style

As you begin the process of planning your career, it is important to keep in mind that a job should not only allow you to use your skills and abilities but also suit your personal needs and values. Career exploration means more than just "looking for a job."

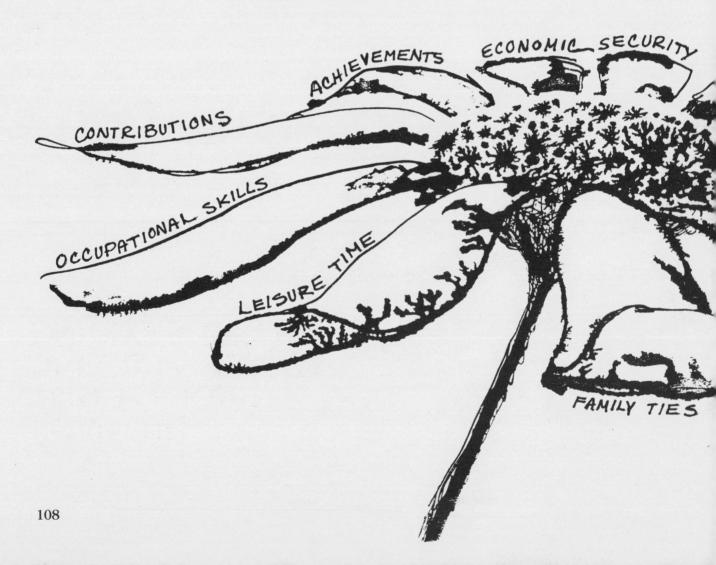

ELEMENTS OF A CAREER

- **PERSONAL VALUES -** Clear sense of what has meaning and importance.
- **OCCUPATIONAL SKILLS -** Well qualified to meet job requirements.
- **ECONOMIC SECURITY -** Adequate income and benefits, opportunities for retraining and promotion.
- **JOB SATISFACTION -** Enjoyable work, safe and pleasant work environment.
- **ACHIEVEMENTS -** Competence in fulfilling responsibilities on the job.
- **CONTRIBUTIONS -** Volunteer work, providing something of value for others.
- **FAMILY TIES -** Relationships that provide emotional support and a sense of belonging.
- **SOCIAL LIFE -** Friendships and activities that contribute to personal satisfaction and spiritual growth.
- **LEISURE TIME -** Hobbies and activities that provide happiness and relaxation.
- **CONTINUING EDUCATION -** Learning experiences that increase knowledge and improve job skills.

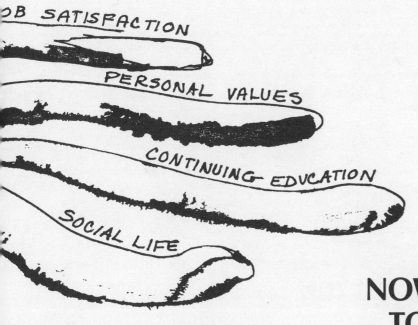

NOW YOU ARE GOING TO BEGIN PLANNING YOUR FUTURE LIFE-STYLE!

What Are My Skills? What Can I Do?

If you were asked to make a list of your skills, you would probably under-estimate yourself and make a short one. You may not think of yourself as having many skills; most people don't. As a matter of fact, you have hundreds of skills. A skill is something you know how to do with things, people, or ideas.

You are probably good at some things but not so good at others. Perhaps you are good at planning homecoming activities, but make a big mess every-time you try to bake a cake. Nobody is good at everything, but everybody can do something.

Every activity that you are involved in from the time you get up in the morning until you go to bed at night requires you to use many skills. Chores at home or part-time jobs involve you in activities that may not be so enjoyable. Nevertheless, such jobs are important because they provide opportunities for you to gain and develop skills.

Hobbies, school activities, and volunteer work also provide opportunities to learn and develop skills. Usually, you enjoy the skills involved in these activities. Whether or not you enjoy the activity, everything that you know how to do is a potential job skill. That is an important point to remember when you begin to make plans for the future.

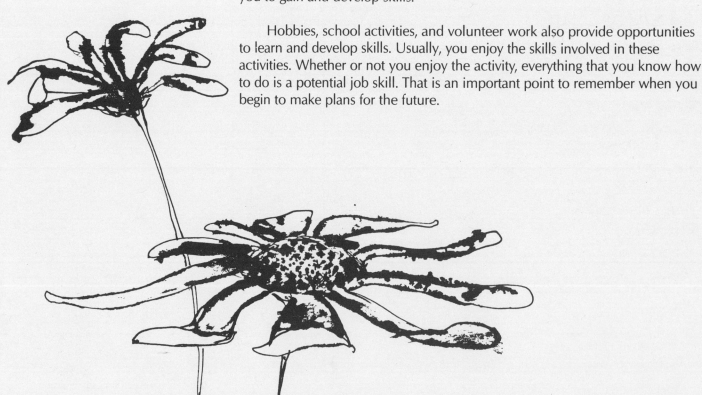

My Skills Inventory

Complete the following inventory by checking the things that you can do. A number of skills have been listed for you just in case you might think they are not important. Even if you feel that you need to improve a skill, check it anyway. You may also add skills that have not been listed.

REMEMBER: When you take inventory, do not leave out anything.

MANAGING PEOPLE/SITUATIONS	SKILLS I HAVE AND ENJOY	SKILLS I WANT TO DEVELOP	SKILLS I WOULD LIKE TO USE ON A JOB
•Giving directions			
•Leading others			
•Making hard decisions			
•Starting new tasks			
•Making changes			
•Taking risks			
•Influencing others			
•Planning			
•Supervising work of others			
•Other _____			

	SKILLS I HAVE AND ENJOY	SKILLS I WANT TO DEVELOP	SKILLS I WOULD LIKE TO USE ON A JOB
TEACHING OTHER PEOPLE			
•Explaining how to do something			
•Leading group discussions			
•Giving information			
•Giving people advice			
•Helping people to help themselves			
•Training others to do things			
•Encouraging people to try			
•Other _____			
CREATING AND PERFORMING			
•Inventing/experimenting			
•Visualizing colors, shapes, images			
•Playing a musical instrument			
•Singing			
•Dancing			
•Acting in a play			
•Writing poems, stories, plays			
•Drawing			
•Painting			
•Modeling			
•Taking photographs			
•Arranging flowers			
•Designing clothes			
•Styling hair			
•Applying makeup on others			
•Other _____			

WORKING WITH NUMBERS/DETAILS

	SKILLS I HAVE AND ENJOY	SKILLS I WANT TO DEVELOP	SKILLS I WOULD LIKE TO USE ON A JOB
•Managing money			
•Doing precision work			
•Keeping deadlines			
•Developing a memory for numbers			
•Counting, calculating, computing			
•Organizing information			
•Following through on assignments			
•Keeping financial records			
•Other _____			

WORKING WITH HANDS

	SKILLS I HAVE AND ENJOY	SKILLS I WANT TO DEVELOP	SKILLS I WOULD LIKE TO USE ON A JOB
•Developing skill in using hands			
•Using machines, tools			
•Repairing things			
•Cleaning and maintenance			
•Gardening			
•Preparing meals			
•Building			
•Typing			
•Operating business machines			
•Driving a vehicle			
•Serving food			
•Painting furniture, house			
•Playing ball			
•Other _____			

113

	SKILLS I HAVE AND ENJOY	SKILLS I WANT TO DEVELOP	SKILLS I WOULD LIKE TO USE ON A JOB
HELPING OTHERS			
•Sharing			
•Expressing warmth			
•Assisting someone in a crisis			
•Working as part of a team			
•Helping others settle disputes			
•Understanding			
•Being sensitive to others' feelings			
•Listening to people's problems			
•Taking care of sick people			
•Taking care of children			
•Other _____			
COMMUNICATING IDEAS			
•Speaking in front of a group			
•Reading			
•Using humor			
•Telling stories			
•Debating			
•Writing letters, reports			
•Selling products			
•Other _____			

WORKING WITH IDEAS/INFORMATION

	SKILLS I HAVE AND ENJOY	SKILLS I WANT TO DEVELOP	SKILLS I WOULD LIKE TO USE ON A JOB
•Gathering information			
•Observing, comparing			
•Finding the cause of a problem			
•Being curious about how things work			
•Concentrating			
•Judging both sides of a situation			
•Using logic			
•Seeing how parts fit together			
•Developing ideas			
•Predicting what will happen			
•Other _____			

You identified your work values in Chapter Three. Now you are going to summarize your work values so that you can use them as you explore occupational choices.

WORK VALUES IMPORTANT TO ME

_____

_____

_____

_____

_____

_____

_____

_____

_____

Skills I Would Like to Use on a Job

Based on your SKILLS INVENTORY, summarize the skills in each of the following categories that you would like to use on a job.

TEACHING OTHER PEOPLE

_____
_____
_____
_____

HELPING OTHERS

_____
_____
_____
_____

CREATING AND PERFORMING

_____
_____
_____
_____

COMMUNICATING IDEAS

_____
_____
_____
_____

MANAGING PEOPLE AND SITUATIONS

_____
_____
_____
_____

WORKING WITH NUMBERS/DETAILS

_____
_____
_____
_____

WORKING WITH IDEAS/INFORMATION

_____
_____
_____
_____

WORKING WITH HANDS

_____
_____
_____
_____

What Are My Options?

The occupational choices that will be available to you in the future, generally, will require skills in one or more of the eight competency areas that you used to identify your skills.

You are now going to use what you have learned about yourself to explore career choices in the following groups:

- •Administrative Support Occupations
- •Construction
- •Engineers, Scientists, and Related Occupations
- •Executive, Administrative, and Managerial
- •Health-related Occupations
- •Marketing and Sales
- •Production Occupations
- •Service Occupations
- •Social Science, Social Services, and Related Occupations
- •Teachers, Counselors, and Related Occupations
- •Transportation and Material Moving Occupations
- •Writers, Artists, and Entertainers

These occupational groups are discussed in the *Occupational Outlook Handbook.* This valuable resource for career exploration can be found in your school library or career center.

The occupations listed on the pages that follow reflect future trends in the job market. The *Occupational Outlook Handbook* contains a description of each job that includes job duties, training and education needed, possibilities for promotions, salaries, what the job outlook will be, and what jobs are related. The salary information on each page represents the lowest and highest salaries nationwide, as indicated in the *Handbook.* Actual salaries for the listed occupations will vary from state to state.

In addition to exploring careers, you will also have the opportunity to meet a number of role models. In their own words, they will share with you their experiences and explain how they achieved success in reaching their goals.

PAULINE CAMPBELL
EQUIPMENT PLANNING MANAGER

My position requires a flexible personality. I am responsible for managing a department that purchases computer related equipment, trains new users of that equipment, and installs and maintains both computers and phones. I also schedule projects, negotiate prices with suppliers, and communicate with company users to determine which equipment and software will work best for them.

I chose this career field because it provides opportunities to work with people. I have always been in user support positions where I provided training services, secretarial support, and new equipment and software support. Although support positions are demanding, they are also rewarding.

When I was in high school, my goal was to become a teacher. After my first part-time job, I found that I enjoyed administrative and support/services work. That experience influenced my career choice. Even though I now have an administrative position, I still have the opportunity to train company employees. Thus, I am able to pursue my interest in teaching.

If I were back in high school, I cannot say that I would change any of my courses. I attended a college preparatory school that had strict course requirements. I do feel that I could have invested more time in my studies.

With the growing popularity of computers, it is becoming much easier to receive computer training. Many companies, temporary employment agencies, and business schools offer training. In addition, the Regional Opportunity Programs (ROP) offer opportunities to train at a company while you are still attending school.

The future outlook for positions in the computer and support field is very good. You can start in a secretarial or clerical position and then advance as you receive additional training. During my six years with Cal Farm, I have received four promotions, with increasing responsibility and salary.

If you are honest with yourself, know what you want to accomplish, and are willing to put forth the extra effort, opportunities for a satisfying career are available for you.

DAPHNE L. RHOE
TELECOMMUNICATIONS SYSTEMS MANAGER

I can recall, not long ago, wondering what I should do with my life after high school graduation. I knew that college was a "must" if I wanted to advance in the world of business. Little did I know then the career that awaited me in the field of telecommunications. Telecommunications means simply communicating at a distance by various means: a telephone at home or in the office, a radio in a police car, or one computer "talking" to another.

As a telecommunications systems manager with the State of California, my primary duties center around developing state telecommunications plans and policies. I meet with our telecommunications engineers on special projects and write reports about integrating the use of technology, the needs of state agencies, and the mandates of legislative and regulatory bodies into state telecommunications policy.

The telecommunications profession chose me as much as I did it. Originally, I had doubts about entering what I felt was a technical field. However, I was intrigued by the challenges as well as encouraged by the career opportunities, especially for women. Fortunately, the State Department of General Services had a very good training program. Much of what I know about this profession was learned on the job. I reinforced my on-the-job training by enrolling in a telecommunications certificate program offered through a local university. This program gave me some much-needed background in specialized areas such as electronics and systems design.

Although a college degree is not absolutely required to enter telecommunications, I strongly recommend

it. A degree can go a long way toward dispelling female stereotypes and improving your credibility on the job. I suggest a degree in telecommunications management, electronics, or management information. I obtained my Bachelor of Science degree in human resources management. I am now working toward my Master of Business Administration degree in telecommunications management.

If you would like to pursue a career in telecommunications, you should check with your high school counselor to make sure that you can take the courses you need to prepare for the college major you have selected. The telecommunications industry is wide open for the Black woman who is serious about a career. After all, there will always be a need to communicate, so there will always be a need for people to design and manage the ever-increasing modes of communication. Why shouldn't you get a piece of the action?

CELESTINE Y. FARMON
SUPERINTENDENT

I work for the California Department of Corrections as superintendent (warden) of a 800 bed women's prison called the Northern California Women's Facility. I am responsible for managing the total operation of this facility, which has approximately 240 staff members and a 12 million dollar budget. My duties include planning, organizing, directing, and coordinating the development of prison programs. In addition, I attend meetings with community leaders and respond to questions regarding the impact of the prison on the quality of life in the community.

My entry into the field of corrections and subsequent promotion are unique. I entered the field as a clerical employee. My goal was to be an executive secretary. Since I was a single parent, being employed was my main concern. Hard work enabled me to advance to my current level. It required self-study, job dedication, and my putting in a lot of extra effort. I advanced in my career by ensuring that I did every job well before I began to consider moving on to another one. When I felt ready to promote, I evaluated the requirements of the new job as well as my skills to be sure that I was confident I could handle the job. I considered every job that I obtained as on-the-job training for the next one.

It took me nineteen years with the Department of Corrections to advance to superintendent. There were and continue to be barriers for women in my field. Being a Black woman made it all the more difficult; but as you can see, it was not impossible.

Perhaps additional education would not have guaranteed my advancement, but I firmly believe it would have provided an edge. Though my education is limited, I am thankful that I was a fairly good student. The classes that have been most helpful for me were public speaking and English, my favorite subject. The ability to communicate, both in writing and orally, has proved to be a valuable asset. Although I have been successful in my career, given the chance to do it all again, I would pursue a higher education.

In the future there will continue to be numerous opportunities for women in the field of corrections. The job options include custodial (correctional officers) and blue collar (plumbers, painters, and electricians) positions. If you choose a career in the field of corrections, you will find that the financial benefits are good.

Given this opportunity to share with you, I stress—get an education—get proud—get determined.

Leena Farmon

120

ADMINISTRATIVE SUPPORT OCCUPATIONS

Bank teller	$10,800-17,200
Bookkeeper and accounting clerk	$11,200-23,200
Computer and peripheral equipment operator	$ 9,500-27,000
Receptionist and information clerks	$ 8,200-17,900
Secretary	$11,458-21,525
Traffic, shipping, and receiving clerks	$ 8,500-25,000
Typist	$ 8,500-25,000

CONSTRUCTION

Blue-collar worker supervisor	$13,200-39,500
Bricklayer and stonemason	$13,500-26,250
Carpenter	$12,250-31,000
Carpet installer	$12,000-35,000
Electrician	$12,000-36,250
Plumber and pipefitter	$11,250-37,050

EXECUTIVE, ADMINISTRATIVE, AND MANAGERIAL

Accountant and auditor	$17,700-60,000
Bank officer and manager	$13,200-52,000
Health services manager	$13,200-52,000
Hotel manager and assistant	$13,000-62,000
Manager and administrator	$16,900-44,200
Personnel/training/labor relations specialist	$13,900-37,680
Purchasing agent	$11,000-40,000

ENGINEERS, SCIENTISTS, AND RELATED OCCUPATIONS

Architect	$15,000-40,000
Biological scientist	$14,390-35,500
Civil Engineer	$26,300-76,200
Computer system analyst	$17,250-43,500
Electrical/electronics engineers	$26,300-76,200
Industrial engineer	$26,300-76,200
Mechanical engineer	$26,300-76,200
Surveyor	$10,500-28,500

MECHANICS AND REPAIRERS

Aircraft mechanic/engine specialist	$25,000-35,000
Automotive/motorcycle mechanics	$16,960-24,640
Automotive body repairer	$28,100 average
Commercial/industrial electronic equipment repairer	$12,500-37,500
Communications equipment mechanic	$12,000,33,400
Computer service technician	$13,500-37,000
Diesel mechanic	$20,640-28,000
General maintenance mechanic	$12,000-24,000
Office machine/cash register servicer	$10,000-36,000

NORMA SKLAREK
ARCHITECT

Even today, the typical mental picture of an architect is a white male in a business suit. This image has been engraved in the public's mind because the overwhelming majority of architects fit this description. When I started to study architecture, most of the professional schools had rigid quotas restricting the admission of Black applicants and females of any color. Under these circumstances, I was fortunate to be admitted into the architecture program at Columbia University in New York. A combination of luck and high grades and test scores made it possible for me to gain admission. Thus, I was able to receive the training I needed in order to pursue my career goals.

For today's high school graduates who may be interested in pursuing an architectural career, the situation is quite different. Universities have no restrictions against women or Blacks entering their programs; in fact, architecture schools are now often seeking out such candidates. In order to apply, you do not need outstanding grades, but they should be good. Your personality traits should include the determination to finish whatever you start. You must be able to stick to a task and try to learn whatever, at first, may seem difficult or incomprehensible. Be prepared for hard work and long hours of studying and really trying without ever giving up. When I was your age, a successful uncle told me that anything worthwhile will be hard work.

College prep courses that are important for architecture are those which teach communication skills such as English, literature, and speech; courses which teach logical thinking and computational skills such as mathematics, especially algebra and geometry; courses which help to train you to follow directions and understand how things work such as science and physics; and courses which train you for esthetic appreciation and drawing such as art, freehand drawing and painting, and mechanical drafting.

The future is bright for you if your goal is to become an architect. Due to our particular life experiences, we have a special gift to add to designing our environment, our homes, offices, factories, educational and recreational buildings. The quality of our living environment will be partly in your hands.

Norma Sklarek

MONIQUE T. GODBOLD
CHEMICAL ENGINEER

I am employed as a chemical engineer at the Sacramento Air Logistics Center, McClellan Air Force Base. I am responsible for quality assurance evaluation and control of aircraft materials. This involves writing material processing procedures and material testing as well as receiving and updating inspections. In addition, I may be assigned a separate workload of individual projects which vary in complexity. The majority of these are process development projects.

My job requires a degree from an accredited four-year college. I obtained my Bachelor of Science degree in chemical engineering from the University of Texas, Austin.

My original intention was to be a premedical student. After talking to a few unemployed premedical students, I learned that they were looking for jobs because they had not yet been admitted to medical school. I decided to pick a major that was marketable in addition to being of interest to me. However, my interest in medicine did not fade. I decided that my chemical engineering emphasis would be biomedical. Thus, I was able to fulfill all of the medical college requirements as well as the required chemical engineering courses. I am currently in the process of applying for medical school.

If you plan to enroll in college as soon as you complete high school, your preparation must begin early. As a matter of fact, it is necessary to start preparing to meet the requirements of the college or university of your choice in the eighth grade. You must be sure to take enough English, math, foreign language, and laboratory

science courses. Try to achieve the highest grade point average obtainable in every one of your subjects, including physical education, since that is averaged into your overall G.P.A. In your junior and senior years, you should take the Scholastic Aptitude Test (SAT). You should begin applying to the schools of your choice during your junior year. Make sure that you inquire about all available types of financial aid such as grants, loans, scholarships, and work study. Above all, be organized, be thorough, and meet all applicable deadlines.

I think that all women should be financially self-supporting and independent. It is imperative that you make yourself marketable. Put yourself in the position to be competitive and to take possession of a good job so that you may live according to the standards of your choice.

Learn to be responsible and accountable for yourself and all of your actions. As long as you keep your direction, stick to your goals, and stay ambitious, you will succeed in life.

Monique T. Godbold

PRODUCTION OCCUPATIONS

Compositor/typesetter	$ 9,900-24,700
Dental laboratory technician	$12,900-21,300
Numerical-control machine-tool operator	$16,660-24,000
Photographic process worker	$ 7,500-18,000
Water/sewage treatment plant operator	$18,700-21,700
Welders and cutter	$20,000-28,000

TRANSPORTATION AND MATERIAL MOVING OCCUPATIONS

Aircraft pilot	$16,000-130,000
Busdriver	$ 7,500-24,250
Truckdriver	$14,420-22,560

TECHNOLOGISTS AND TECHNICIANS

Computer programmer	$14,250-39,000
Electrical/electronics technicians	$11,458-34,700
Engineering technician	$11,458-37,000
Legal assistant	$14,400-27,700
Science technician	$11,458-37,000
Tool programmer, numerical control	$10,413-24,000

MARKETING AND SALES

Cashier	$ 6,700-17,500
Manufacturers' sales worker	$12,500-44,200
Real estate agent and broker	varies
Retail sales worker	$ 6,700-25,500
Securities/financial services sales worker	$10,800-156,000
Travel agent	$10,000-20,000
Wholesale trade sales worker	$12,000-42,000

WRITERS, ARTISTS, AND ENTERTAINERS

Dancer and choreographer	varies
Designer	$10,500-40,500
Graphic and fine artists	$13,000-26,000
Musician	$13,350-38,900
Photographer/camera operator	$ 9,000-42,800
Public relations specialist	$13,500-52,000
Writer and editor	$ 9,700-60,000

LINDA TANNER
STATIONARY ENGINEER

I am completing a four-year program as a stationary engineer apprentice. The program includes on-the-job training and two years of coursework at a community college. My job duties require me to operate, maintain, and repair machinery that heats and cools over twenty-one State of California buildings. In addition, I am enrolled in mechanical electrical technology at Sacramento City College. I will receive a certificate when I complete my coursework.

I chose a career in the field of engineering because of the challenges it offers and the opportunities for upward mobility. There were very few women in this field when I made my decision. Even though I had to take a demotion in order to get into the apprentice program, I felt that it would be worth it in the long run.

As a woman in a nontraditional occupation, I do have my ups and downs. Most of my coworkers have accepted the fact that a woman will be working alongside of them. As long as I make an effort to carry out my responsibilities and keep my attention focused on my job, I get along well. There are still some men, however, who have not accepted my presence. They feel intimidated by a woman in a nontraditional job. They fear that their promotional opportunities will be limited if they have to compete with a woman.

The classes that I took in high school were not helpful in preparing me for my job. Classes that would have been helpful were offered at my school. Unfortunately, girls were not encouraged to take "boys' classes" such as metal shop, mechanical shop, or auto shop. If I were back in high school, I would insist on taking these classes so that I could develop my mechanical abilities.

When I was in high school, I wanted to be a social worker. Later, I discovered that there were many social workers but not enough jobs. I decided to pursue my interest in a career field that would provide opportunities for training and job mobility.

It is important for me as a single Black woman to be self-sufficient so that I can maintain an acceptable standard of living. My nontraditional blue collar job provides the financial resources to enable me to purchase my own home and to be independent.

Future opportunities will be available for girls who take "boys' classes" in order to prepare for blue collar jobs. Exciting challenges and financial security can be yours if you choose to pursue a nontraditional career.

Linda A. Tanner

VALERIE WEIR
ELECTRONICS TECHNICIAN

As an electronics technician trainee with the State of California, my typical day begins with pulling cable into the Capitol Building offices, putting together or repairing radios, troubleshooting the legislative monitoring system, and setting up public address systems for rallies at the Capitol.

Electronics was not my first career choice. I wanted to be a secretary, marry the young and fine-looking boss, and have him take care of me. I took typing and shorthand and went, eventually, to secretarial school. By then, I had become an "independent woman" and decided that as a secretary I could get my foot in the door and work my way up.

Well, I did get one step above the level of secretary while working with the state; however, in my department that was as far as I could advance. I took a long hard look at my career. I considered the things I liked doing such as tinkering with mechanical objects. Then I looked up the specifications for the classes that matched my interests.

Next, I talked to someone in the field of telecommunications so that I could learn about working conditions, preparation and qualifications necessary, and job opportunities. I was told about cases of male resentment toward females who were breaking into the field. That did not change my mind. Based on the information that I had obtained, I enrolled in a two-year electronics program at a local college.

The hardest part of getting into electronics was finding a supervisor willing to take a chance on me. I started looking before I finished my program. By the time I finished, I had a job where I could use my training. Electronics is a great field for females. I have not encountered problems because I have a strong sense of self.

My experience as a high school student government organization rep helped me to present myself favorably to prospective employers. Because my experience was so valuable, my advice to you is participate in student government and clubs. These activities help you learn how to sell yourself and your ideas. You also learn how to use appropriate language and build the self-confidence that you will need to enter the job market.

Enroll in algebra and geometry. Yes, there are practical uses for these subjects—in electronics, for example. Do not be afraid to get in there and give it your best. I did not do that when I was in high school. If I had the chance to go back, I would try to do my best. A career in electronics is an excellent choice if you like to tinker. You can expect a good salary and job security in a field that will continue to grow in the future.

ARLENE STEVENS
TELEVISION PROGRAM DIRECTOR

As director of program development at KEEF TV-68, Los Angeles, I manage some of the exciting activities that result in what people see on our television station everyday. My main job is to find or put together television programs that people will enjoy, programs that will help them learn about different subjects, and programs that provide information about what is going on in the city, state, and around the world. I chose this job because I wanted to be a part of an educational television station that would put on new kinds of programs for people of different races, languages, and ages.

When I was a high school student in New York, the two subjects that I liked and did well in were Spanish and English. I was in an honors English class and studied college-level Spanish. I also worked as a reporter/writer for the school newspaper. These classes and activities turned out to be very helpful to me on the job.

If I were back in high school, I would work harder in subjects that I did not have as much interest in, such as math and the sciences. You never know where, when, or how you might be able to use what you have learned. That was true for me since I did not know exactly what kind of job I wanted. At one time, I thought about working at the United Nations as a translator, translating speeches from Spanish to English. But, one thing was for sure—I wanted to go to college to study more.

In college I studied Spanish, English, education and other subjects. After teaching at a college, I became interested in and studied television while I did volunteer work at different television stations. Three things

helped me to be ready to work as the director of program development: my high school and college classes and work experience; the love and support of my family and friends; and the fact that I really wanted to do this kind of work. I think that it is important and I enjoy it. We spend a lot of time watching television. However, we do not see very many Black women working at television stations, either in the offices or on the television shows. Some people feel that we do not have an equal chance to get these kinds of jobs and to show our talent. There may be different reasons for that. I never let any of those reasons stop me from trying to get the job I wanted or stop me from doing my job well. The future in my career field can be bright; you can begin preparing yourself for it now. Because there are so few women in television management, there is room to enter, grow, help in some way, and let others know it can be done.

Arlene Stevens

MONICA CROOKS
GENERAL DENTIST

As a general dentist, I am licensed to perform procedures in all dental specialties. On a typical day, I perform clinical examinations, read diagnostic x-rays, provide basic dental fillings and root canal fillings, fabricate gold and porcelain crowns, make dentures, clean teeth, apply and adjust braces, and perform surgical procedures. I enjoy my work and I also enjoy owning my own business.

I pursued a career in the field of dentistry because I excelled in math and science and was advised by my college professors to consider a career in one of the medical professions. I chose dentistry because of the independence that it allows. Dentistry is a self-owned, self-initiated, and self-controlled business.

In order to learn more about the dental profession, I volunteered to assist a dentist in my community. I was blessed to work with a dentist who encouraged me and gave me sound advice. I was favorably impressed by him because he took great pride in providing the highest quality service for his patients. I decided to concentrate vigorously on the pursuit of a dental degree.

When I was in high school, my central focus was on going to college. However, I gave no thought to what I would study in college. Rather I concentrated on making A's and figured that since I was a good student, everything would fall into place automatically. I was blessed to be accepted into all of the dental schools to which I applied. I had a 3.9 grade point average and a host of letters of recommendation to my credit.

I attended an undergraduate university for four years and graduated with a Bachelor of Science degree in biology. I completed the four year course of dental training at the University of California, Los Angeles, School of Dentistry. I achieved what I wanted to achieve and quite probably so will you.

If I had to complete high school all over again, I would strive to excel even more in basic studies such as English and math. Effective communication, both written and verbal, is essential to success in business. It is important to learn all that you can about computers. In addition, learn how to type and how to take shorthand; these skills are quite helpful for achieving success in college.

Learn as much as you can about the career field you are interested in, whether it is dentistry or some other profession. For example, talk to people in the profession and find out why they became involved. Take advantage of opportunities that are available to you; never before have there been so many opportunities for advancement for young Black students. Pursue high goals and strive to be successful.

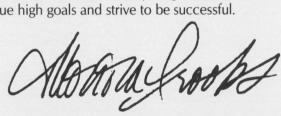

ALICIA KIM DIXON
PUBLIC HEALTH TRAINEE

At a very early age, I was taught that a college education is important because it not only offers expertise in a particular field but also provides personal growth, independence, and self-fulfillment.

I was the first in my family to attend college, so we were not familiar with the application process. My high school counselors did not provide much information and support, but my math and science teachers were quite helpful. As a result of their guidance, I was accepted at the University of California, San Diego, as a biology major.

Unfortunately, my family and I could not afford the fees required to attend UCSD. We overcame this stumbling block by applying for and receiving financial aid that included loans, grants, and scholarships. If you apply for college, be aware of the financial aid deadlines and make sure you meet them.

Before attending UCSD, I knew that most of the students were white. What I was not sure of was how I would be treated or how I would react in this new and very different environment. I soon realized that I would be treated like any other student, but I was not just any other student. I was unique; in most of my classes, I was the only Black or sometimes one of only three Black students in a lecture hall of 300 students. Therefore, I had to overcome feelings of insecurity in order to be a successful student.

I reached my goal of earning a Bachelor of Arts degree in microbiology by studying hard and by building strong ties with other students. My participation in the Black Student Union gave me positive reinforcement and the encouragement to stay in school.

When I graduated from high school, I had plans to become a physician. After being exposed to many other career options, my interest shifted to the field of public health. I am working toward completion of the requirements for the master's degree in public health.

If I had the opportunity to trade places with you today, I would learn as much as I could about biology and Afro-American history by visiting a variety of libraries and by utilizing community resources. Unfortunately, while in high school, I used the library only for special assignments. While attending UCSD, I spent fifty percent of my time in the library. Learn from my mistake; develop good study habits while in high school.

I certainly hope that you will rely on your own motivation and self-discipline to help you complete your education. Make education a priority.

Alicia K Dixon

HEALTH RELATED OCCUPATIONS

Dental hygienist $12,860- 22,000
Dentist $26,400- 95,000
Dietitian and nutritionist $14,390- 28,000
Dispensing optician $15,000- 30,000
Electrocardiograph technician $12,000- 25,000
Licensed practical nurse $11,000- 20,000
Medical record technician $13,200- 20,000
Occupational therapist $17,820- 33,000
Optometrist $27,000- 55,000
Physician $20,000-152,000
Physical therapist $17,820- 35,000
Physician assistant $17,800- 39,000
Podiatrist $26,380- 50,000
Radiological technician $14,400- 25,900
Recreational therapist $14,500- 23,400
Registered nurse $15,000- 37,300
Respiratory therapist $13,000- 23,100
Speech pathologist and audiologist $19,800- 34,900
Veterinarian $26,380- 50,000

SERVICE OCCUPATIONS

Chef, cook, except short order .... $ 7,600-40,000
Childcare worker .... $ 6,700-15,600
Correction officer $14,400-34,000
Cosmetologist/related worker .... $ 6,000-20,000
Dental assistant $11,458-15,200
Firefighting occupation $17,300-52,300
Guard .... $ 6,700-18,480
Janitor and cleaner .... $ 6,700-19,350
Medical assistant .... $ 7,000-15,000
Nursing aide/psychiatric aide .... $ 7,000-17,000
Police officer and detective $18,000-30,900
Waiter and waitress .... $ 6,600-15,500

TEACHERS, COUNSELORS AND RELATED OCCUPATIONS

Adult/vocational education teacher .... $ 9,500-36,000
Counselor .... $27,593 (Average)
Kindergarten/elementary school teacher .... $23,092 (Average)
Librarian $17,232-31,530
Secondary school teachers .... $24,276 (Average)
College and university faculty .... $31,000 (Average)

SOCIAL SCIENCE, SOCIAL SERVICES, AND RELATED OCCUPATIONS

Economist $17,800-52,000
Lawyer $10,000-88,000
Protestant minister $18,000-25,000
Psychologist $14,400-48,000
Recreation worker $15,000-26,000
Social worker $15,700-30,800

LILLIAN BROWN
POLICE OFFICER

My duties as a reserve police officer for the Sacramento City Policy Department range from traffic control to boat control. On a typical workday, I am mainly involved in traffic control. This requires me to direct traffic at designated intersections in various parts of the city. When you're out there, you really have to think on your feet because you have the safety of motorists as well as pedestrians in your hands.

In addition to directing traffic, I write citations for parking violators and moving violators. There is more to writing a citation for a moving violation than just asking for a license. Our number one priority is officer safety.

Shortly after graduating from high school, I began working for the State of California as a secretary. Because of my interest in law enforcement, I decided to contact the Sacramento City Police Department to find out about employment opportunities. To qualify, I had to pass a background investigation, an interview, and a physical exam. After completing three months of training at the Sacramento Police Academy, I was sworn in as a reserve officer.

I am certain that some of my high school activities helped to prepare me for my chosen career field. I was a cheer leader and a member of the drill team. I also worked on the journalism staff, ran track, and played volleyball. All of these activities provided me with skills in getting along with people. In addition, I had good references when I began to seek employment.

I suggest that you participate in student activities because they help you to develop positive peer relationships. You should also study a foreign language, preferably Spanish. Proficiency in Spanish is a plus, especially in law enforcement.

The field of law enforcement offers many career opportunities. If you choose to become a police officer, you can begin your career after you graduate from high school. An alternative is to first complete two years of college to obtain a background in criminal justice and social science.

Becoming a reserve officer is the best thing that has happened to me. I think if I had to do it all again, I would take the same route because of the many opportunities for future advancement.

LaRUTH McREYNOLDS
ADMINISTRATIVE LAW JUDGE

My position is that of Deputy Commissioner with the State of California Board of Prison Terms. As an administrative law judge, I review offenders' behavior and assess penalties for misconduct.

My work responsibilities require me to demonstrate the ability to get along with people and to make wise decisions. I began my career in the field of criminal justice in a clerical position. The longer I remained in the field, the more my interest increased. Therefore, I decided to seek opportunities to move up the career ladder. My efforts were quite successful. I was promoted from an entry position to supervisor and administrator. Eventually, I became a hearing officer for the State Narcotic Parole Authority and then moved on to the Board of Prison Terms.

I am satisfied with my career choice because I am able to use both my administrative training and the skills that I acquired in college. I received a Bachelor of Arts degree in social science/social service and my master's degree work was in public administration.

As a Black female, I have had many opportunities to be a "first." For example, I was the first female to hold the training manager position in a male prison. I had been denied the position a year before I was hired because, prior to the affirmative action laws of the 1970s, females were not hired to fill such positions. I have experienced numerous problems related to being a female in a nontraditional position. They have challenged me to be my best. The results have been greatly rewarding. I am particularly grateful to be able to offer a perspective that is different from the otherwise limited view that often exists in this society.

While in high school, I developed good study habits; I enjoyed reading and science. I recall being placed in an accelerated English class. My goal then was to become a physical education teacher and to attend one of the Southern Black colleges. A course I took in typing and shorthand enabled me to obtain my first job after high school.

Looking back, if I were in high school, I would participate in a debate club and enroll in technical skill electives and enrichment courses. In addition, I would put diligent effort into qualifying for scholarships.

Discipline and determination are required for a successful career in criminal justice. The field offers a wide variety of career options for you to explore. Never be limited by the idea that someone like you has never done the job before. If it can be done by anyone, then you can do it.

LaRuth Boddie McReynolds

DONNA M. SMITH
COLLEGE DEAN

My position as Dean of the Mathematics and Engineering Division at American River College, Sacramento, requires me to rely heavily on my problem-solving and communication skills. I attend meetings, schedule classes, appropriate the budget, work with committees, and administer academic programs for a staff of fifty people. In addition, I am the college representative for the Mathematical Association of America.

Prior to becoming dean of the division, I was a mathematics instructor. My primary responsibility was to teach four or five classes each semester. These included arithmetic, algebra, trigonometry, statistics, calculus, and differential equations. Many students, especially females, expressed a fear of math. In order to make math less scary for them, I provided a workshop on math anxiety every semester. I also served on a curricular committee that helped to develop a pre-calculus course designed to better prepare students for the calculus sequence. For a year, I was director of the Math Learning Center, which served 1,500 students.

When I went to college, I wanted to become a chemical engineer. As it turned out, math was easier for me. I changed my major to mathematics and earned my Bachelor of Arts degree at Pomona College, and my Master of Arts degree at the University of California, Berkeley. Throughout my college years, I received academic scholarships. In addition, I received the Moncrief Astronomy Prize, a cash award for students who demonstrated proficiency in observatory work.

During my undergraduate years, I was able to divide my time between academics and sports. I was a serious student as well as a member of the varsity track team. I won first place in the Southern California Intercollegiate Athletic Conference (SCIAS) for the discus two years in a row. I held the SCIAC record for the discus in 1980.

I was the first person in my immediate family to graduate from college. It never occurred to me that because I was a girl I should not study math. All of my grammar and high school math teachers were women. As a matter of fact, my 7th and 8th grade algebra teacher, a Black woman, served as my role model.

There are very few training programs and occupations that do not require basic math skills. Therefore, girls should begin taking math classes in junior high school. Contrary to the myth, math is not for boys only. If you enroll in a math class and it becomes difficult for you, do not give up and drop the class. Stay in there and get the help that you need from your teacher or a tutor. You will not regret it. A background in mathematics will open the door to many career opportunities.

Donna M. Smith

133

As you were learning about various occupations, you had the opportunity to meet some dynamic women who are actively involved in their careers. Perhaps learning about their experiences has encouraged you to begin thinking about the kind of work you might want to do in the future. In order to explore further, you will need to spend some time in your school's library and career center. Ask to see the *Occupational Outlook Handbook*, which was the source of the salary information presented on the preceding pages. In addition, you should request reference books, pamphlets, brochures, and other materials on the careers that you want to explore. This will be a good time to practice being assertive. You need the information, so do not be afraid to ask for it.

Use the "Career Exploration" form on the following page to record the specific information that you need in order to see how your occupational choices fit your skills, interests, and values. Be sure to refer to the work values and skills that you listed on pages 115 and 116.

CAREER EXPLORATION

Job Title: _____

_____

Salary: _____

Duties: _____

_____

_____

_____

Job Outlook: _____

_____

_____

_____

Training/Qualifications: _____

_____

_____

_____

_____

Working Conditions: _____

_____

_____

_____

_____

MY ACADEMIC PREPARATION

Courses: _____

_____

_____

_____

Activities: _____

_____

_____

_____

My Work Values: _____

_____

_____

_____

My Skills: _____

_____

_____

_____

Conversation with a Role Model

While exploring career options, you have learned a lot about yourself. You have also learned about traditional and nontraditional jobs that are expected to be available when you graduate from high school. You are now beginning to think seriously about two or three occupational choices. You probably would like to know more about what it is like to work on the jobs that you have chosen. One of the best ways to find out what a job is like is to talk directly with someone who is already doing that job. People like to talk about their work, especially with young people. A conversation with a role model can provide helpful information that you can use to make decisions about your future career.

This phase of your career exploration will take you beyond the boundaries of your school and maybe even beyond the boundaries of your neighborhood. You will need to identify two women working in career fields that you are interested in and arrange to talk with them about their work. Your counselor, your teachers, and your adult relatives and friends can probably help you find women to interview and also assist you in setting up appointments with those women. Note in Lisa's story how she asserted herself and got the help and information she needed.

LISA'S STORY

When Lisa decided that she wanted to be an electrician, she wasn't quite sure that this was a wise choice for a female. She was quite efficient in handling the lighting and sound equipment for school plays and assemblies. In fact, she had learned how to make minor repairs safely. Nevertheless, the thought of her becoming a self-employed electrician seemed a bit unrealistic.

One day Lisa decided to discuss her career interests with the drama teacher, Mrs. Miller. Much to her surprise, Mrs. Miller did not try to discourage her; instead, she assured Lisa that there were female electricians working in their own city. In fact, one of them had recently signed a contract to install the wiring in the new community theater where Mrs. Miller directs a children's drama group. She gave Lisa the electrician's name and telephone number and urged her to call and ask for an appointment. Later that same day, Lisa called Apex Electrical Service and made an appointment with the owner, Ms. Alice Fairley.

When Lisa went in to talk with Ms. Fairley, she gained valuable information as well as reassurance that it was okay for a female to consider a career as an electrician. Lisa's conversation with her role model went smoothly because she listened carefully and took notes. She had a list of questions to guide her so that she could make wise use of Ms. Fairley's time.

On the following pages are questions that will guide you through your conversations with your role models.

Conversation #1

Name of role model _____ *Date* _____

Job title _____

• *Why did you choose your present occupation?* _____
_____

• *How long have you worked in this field?* _____

• *What is your work schedule?* _____
_____

• *What duties do you perform on a typical day?* _____
_____
_____

• *What is the salary range for jobs like yours?* _____

• *What do you like about your job?* _____
_____
_____

• *What do you dislike about your job?* _____
_____
_____

• *What barriers have you had to overcome?* _____
_____

• *What training did you receive to prepare yourself for this job?* _____

• *Which high school courses were helpful to you?* _____
_____

• *What student activities were helpful to you?* _____
_____

•*What did you plan to do after high school?* _____
_____

•*If you could go back to high school and start over, what would you do differently?* _____
_____

•*Do you expect jobs like yours to be available ten years from now?* _____
_____

•*If I tried to get a job like yours, what barriers would I face?* _____
_____

•*What opportunities would be available for me in your field?* _____
_____

•*What words would you use to describe yourself?* _____
_____

•*My impression of my role model:* _____
_____
_____
_____
_____
_____
_____
_____

Conversation #2

Name of role model _____ Date _____

Job title _____

• *Why did you choose your present occupation?* _____

_____

• *How long have you worked in this field?* _____

• *What is your work schedule?* _____

_____

• *What duties do you perform on a typical day?* _____

_____

_____

• *What is the salary range for jobs like yours?* _____

• *What do you like about your job?* _____

_____

_____

• *What do you dislike about your job?* _____

_____

_____

• *What barriers have you had to overcome?* _____

_____

• *What training did you receive to prepare yourself for this job?* _____

_____

• *Which high school courses were helpful to you?* _____

_____

• *What student activities were helpful to you?* _____

_____

•*What did you plan to do after high school?* _____

_____

•*If you could go back to high school and start over, what would you do differently?* _____

_____

•*Do you expect jobs like yours to be available ten years from now?* _____

_____

•*If I tried to get a job like yours, what barriers would I face?* _____

_____

•*What opportunities would be available for me in your field?* _____

_____

•*What words would you use to describe yourself?* _____

_____

•*My impression of my role model:* _____

_____

_____

_____

_____

_____

_____

_____

PART III

Your sense of self-esteem and your ability to make wise use of your knowledge, skills, and resources will determine how successful you are in reaching your goals for the future.

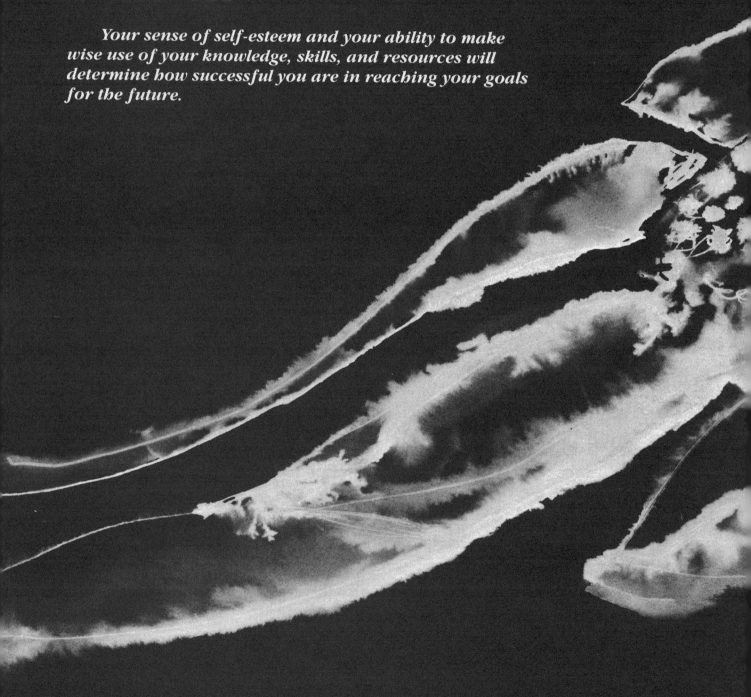

How Do I Get There?

Chapter Six

Reality: What is actual or true; what exists at any given time; what one perceives as actual or true.

REALITY AND RESPONSIBILITY

The freedom to weave in and out of a make-believe world is one of the advantages of childhood. Children are permitted to pretend and play many roles; that is one of the ways they learn about life in the adult world. They can make decisions and behave in ways that would be unacceptable if they were adolescents or adults. Children can blame their mistakes on someone else—a brother or sister, the cat, or a make-believe playmate. Usually, they can get away with it.

One of the most difficult challenges related to growing up is that when you are a teenager, blaming others is no longer cute; it is childish and irresponsible. The present stage of your life, adolescence, is a transition period —a bridge between the world of make-believe and the world of adulthood and responsibility. As you continue your growth toward maturity, you will learn that freedom and responsibility are related. In other words, when you make decisions, you have to accept responsibility for the outcome of your decisions.

Much of what you have learned in your search for self can help to guide you as you make decisions in your daily life. Your values, beliefs, and needs can help you set priorities so that you can act on the basis of what is important and what is best for you.

DECISIONS . . . . . DECISIONS . . . . . DECISIONS

What color blouse should I wear today?

Should I enroll in a word processing class?

Should I study tonight or watch TV?

Should I have sex with my boyfriend?

Every decision, no matter what it concerns, requires you to do some thinking. Of course, some decisions require more serious thinking than others. Generally, it is necessary to go through a thought process that requires you to ask yourself a series of questions:

- •What is the decision to be made?
- •Who and what are involved?
- •Where and when will it happen?
- •Why and how will it happen?
- •What knowledge do I have to make this decision?
- •What is most important to me?
- •What beliefs and values do I have to help me make this decision?
- •What will I actually do?
- •When and where?

After the decision is made, you evaluate the outcome and ask yourself:

- •Did I go against my beliefs and values?
- •Did I base my decision on what I actually knew?
- •Would I do the same thing again?
- •How is this decision going to affect my life?

What Will Happen If I . . . ?

Think about some situations that you have been involved in recently or something that could happen in the future that would require you to make a decision. Choose two situations and use the thought process outlined below to guide your decisions and to evaluate their outcomes. You will have to use your imagination in order to complete the decision-making process.

SITUATION #1:

_____

_____

_____

_____

• *The decision I must make* _____

_____

• *People and action involved* _____

_____

• *Why should I do this?* _____

_____

• *How I should do this* _____

_____

• *Knowledge I can use* _____

_____

• *What is most important to me?* _____

_____

•My beliefs and values _____

_____

•What could happen?

1. _____

2. _____

3. _____

•My decision: I am going to _____

_____

•When _____ *Where* _____

RESULTS:
WHAT HAPPENED AS A RESULT OF MY DECISION?

_____

_____

_____

_____

_____

_____

MY EVALUATION:

•Did I go against my values and beliefs? _____

_____

•Did I rely on what I knew? _____

_____

•Would I do it again? _____

_____

•How is it going to affect my life? _____

_____

_____

SITUATION #2

_____

_____

_____

_____

•*The decision I must make* _____

_____

•*People and action involved* _____

_____

•*Why should I do this?* _____

_____

•*How I should do this* _____

_____

•*Knowledge I can use* _____

_____

•*What is most important to me?* _____

_____

•*My beliefs and values* _____

_____

•*What could happen?*

1. _____

2. _____

3. _____

•*My decision: I am going to* _____

_____

•*When* _____ *Where* _____

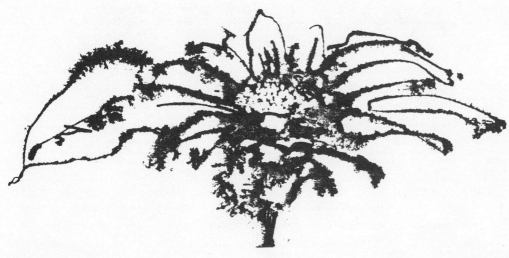

RESULTS:
WHAT HAPPENED AS A RESULT OF MY DECISION?

_____
_____
_____
_____
_____
_____

MY EVALUATION:

•*Did I go against my values and beliefs?* _____
_____

•*Did I rely on what I knew?* _____
_____

•*Would I do it again?* _____
_____

•*How is it going to affect my life?* _____
_____
_____

Decisions About Marriage

During your career exploration you discovered many occupational choices that you can consider as you plan your future life-style. There are also choices related to marriage for you to consider: when to marry, whom to marry, or if you should remain single. Who you are—your personal values, interests, and needs will shape your expectations and influence your decisions about marriage.

A woman who chooses to marry makes a commitment to share her life in a relationship that requires her to blend her needs, values, and interests with those of her husband. The reality of marriage involves more than romance and how well you and your boyfriend look together. More is required than flowers, beautiful gowns, gifts, and a honeymoon.

Marriage requires:
•Patience with each other's faults
•Mutual respect
•Tolerance of individual differences
•Loyalty to the relationship
•The ability to be friends with one another
•Love and devotion even when your marriage partner is not
 so lovable
•Endurance when there is stress and problems to solve
•Sufficient income to meet basic needs
•Sacrifices to support and train children who become a part of
 the marriage

These are just some of the challenges and responsibilities that a woman faces when she commits herself to a marriage.

Decisions about marriage are often related to career plans. For example, a woman who chooses a career field that requires a college degree or extensive training may decide to delay marriage until after she has completed her training. This would enable her to devote full time to her studies and training so that she can be well-prepared to pursue her occupational goals. A career that requires a woman to travel a great deal or to spend long hours on the job may also cause her to delay marriage.

There are a number of other reasons why a woman may decide to delay marriage. Probably the reason most familiar to you is the need to wait until one is mature enough to select an appropriate mate and take on the responsibilities related to marriage.

A woman may choose to remain single because her career provides the economic security that she desires. Her hobbies, community and church activities, and the freedom to travel can contribute to a satisfying life-style. In addition to meeting personal goals, she can make worthwhile contributions to her community. A woman who chooses this life-style must be prepared, however, to handle pressure from family members and friends who expect her to get married.

Often a woman may be single because of the lack of suitable men to select from, a disappointing relationship, death of her husband, separation, or divorce. A woman who is single because of one of these reasons can involve herself in activities and hobbies that contribute to her personal growth. As a result, she can gain satisfaction and maintain her self-esteem.

Perhaps at this stage in your growth toward maturity, you feel that decisions about marriage are far off in the future. Nevertheless, you do have some ideas, dreams, and expectations about getting married. You are aware of the experiences of your parents, relatives, and friends. You also receive many media messages. For example, you see magazine ads that show brides in beautiful gowns. You also see soap operas and movies on television that depict lavish weddings and receptions. You are influenced by the behavior of others and by the messages from the media. Take some time to explore your thoughts about marriage.

In the future, when you are ready to make some serious decisions, you may want to look back at the ideas that you recorded on this day.

My Options:
To Marry or Remain Single

•*My definition of marriage:* _____

_____

_____

_____

•*Why I would marry:* _____

_____

_____

_____

•*The kind of man I would like to marry:* _____

_____

_____

_____

•*Why I would remain single:* _____

_____

_____

_____

•*What my family expects me to do:* _____

_____

_____

_____

•*Today is* _____ . *I am* _____ *years old.*
        month   *day*   *year*

The Challenge of Parenthood

One of the most important decisions you will ever make is the decision to become a parent. When you choose to become a parent, you take on the responsibility for another human being. You need to explore the realities and the challenges of parenthood before you make the decision to give life to another human being.

When you picture in your mind the image of a baby, what do you see?

Write a brief description of a baby.

•*A baby is* _____

_____

_____

_____

_____

_____

_____

_____

_____

_____

NOW CONSIDER THIS DESCRIPTION:

Babies are little people who need lots of love and attention. They do not, however, give back love in ways that their parents may want or crave. Babies do not understand the difference between night and day, and they do not know the difference between right and wrong. Babies are demanding; they do not care about anything or anybody except themselves and their needs. When they are wet, hungry, sleepy, sick, angry, or uncomfortable—in any way—they cry, scream, kick, and scratch in order to have their needs met. Babies are totally dependent on their parents twenty-four hours a day.

Are you ready to assume total responsibility for one of these little people?

Parenthood requires maturity and the willingness to make sacrifices without expecting much in return. Perhaps the greatest reward that parents receive is the satisfaction of knowing that little persons, like the ones just described, can turn out to be loving, self-confident, and responsible human beings. Being a parent is really a matter of trial and error. As you know, there are no required courses in school on how to be an effective parent. **The reality of being a parent requires one to learn on the job many skills and responsibilities.** These are just a few of the things parents must do for their children.

- Provide adequate prenatal care and good early nutrition.
- Provide adequate medical and dental care.
- Provide a secure, loving home environment.
- Instill basic values such as those discussed in Chapter One.
- Maintain consistent discipline and authority.
- Give unconditional love.
- Demand respect and give respect.
- Keep lines of communication open.
- Monitor all school and social activities from preschool through twelfth grade.
- Have clear expectations for behavior and achievement.
- Serve as role models for discipline and responsible behavior.

Underlying all of these responsibilities is the requirement to provide financial support, which totals thousands of dollars by the time a baby becomes a high school graduate. How much does it cost?

Example:

A baby girl is born in 1988; she will be 18 years old by the year 2006. Assume that it will cost approximately $6,500 a year to provide food, clothing, housing, health care, education, and recreation for her until she graduates from high school. How much will she cost her parents?

18 years x $6,500 = $117,000

ARE YOU READY FOR THE CHALLENGES OF PARENTHOOD?

Diane's Story

Prom night was so exciting for Diane. She was chairperson of the Junior Prom committee. Everything—the music, the food, the decorations—seemed just perfect. To top it off, her date was Eric, the most popular boy in the class. She was so glad that she had persuaded her parents to let her go to the breakfast that Eric and some of his friends had planned.

The breakfast was not what Diane had expected. It turned out to be a party at a motel. There were a few snacks and lots of beer and wine. Because Diane trusted Eric and liked him a lot, she did not object to staying. He encouraged her to drink some beer so that she could relax and have fun. She was not accustomed to drinking, so the beer made her feel dizzy.

Eric took Diane outside to get some fresh air. They soon walked over to his car and got into the back seat. Eric began to kiss her and pretty soon convinced her to go all the way with him. She thought it would be okay just this one time. He assured her that nothing could happen to her because both of them had drunk a lot of beer.

Diane's perfect prom night turned out to be a major disaster. It is now the summer before her senior year and instead of shopping for new school clothes, she is shopping for maternity clothes. She does not understand how it happened.

Did Diane make a decision to get pregnant?
Your answer: ___ Yes   ___ No

Review what happened and give reasons for your answer.

_____

_____

_____

_____

Compare your answer with the following:

Diane made three decisions that led to what happened to her.
1. She decided to stay at the party, even though it was not what she had expected.
2. She decided to drink beer, which she was not accustomed to drinking.
3. She agreed to have sex with Eric.

In essence, Diane had three opportunities to say **NO** and thereby prevent what happened to her. Obviously, she needed to know how to apply the decision-making process that you have just learned how to use.

As you can see from what happened to Diane, the decision to become a teenage parent can change the course of your life. Future plans for higher education and a career can be completely wiped out by one unwise decision.

WHAT ELSE DOES DIANE HAVE TO LOOK FORWARD TO AS A TEENAGE MOTHER?
•She is less likely to complete her education.
•She is less likely to be employed.
•If she works, she will probably earn low wages.
•She is less likely to get married.
•She will have less time for social activities.
•Her baby is more likely to be underweight and to have health problems, a disease, or a physical disability.
•She is more likely to have physical problems because of her immature body structure.
•She may be too immature to provide the care and intellectual stimulation that her baby will need.

WOULD YOU LIKE TO TRADE PLACES WITH DIANE?

Preparing for the Unexpected

Exploring the reality of the adult world has made you aware of many challenges and responsibilities that you have to face. You learned from the role models that in order to be successful in their careers, it was necessary for them to overcome many barriers. Fortunately, adults have their maturity and experience to rely on when they have to make decisions. Still, they are not always prepared to face barriers or unexpected events, such as:

•Economic changes that cause the loss of a job
•Discrimination based on race
•Discrimination based on sex
•Illness or death of a parent, wife or husband, or child
•Lack of child care
•Lack of transportation
•Loss of property due to theft or fire

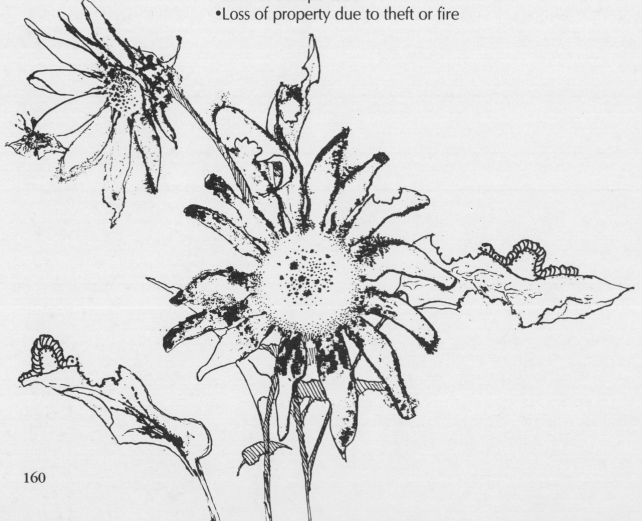

Frequently, situations such as these make it difficult for adults to handle family responsibilities or to perform their jobs efficiently. In order to deal with barriers or unexpected events, they use various strategies such as those that follow:

Rely on community resources.
•Go to state employment agency for job referrals or unemployment benefits.
•Use services of church day-care programs.
•Get family assistance from local welfare agency.

Acquire new skills or knowledge.
•Enroll in vocational training or college.
•Complete high school diploma requirements.
•Obtain on-the-job training.

Change behavior or life-style.
•Provide care for sick relative.
•Relocate to accept a new job.
•Become head of family because of separation or divorce.

In Chapter Four you learned about barriers that you may face as a student. In addition, you developed strategies for overcoming them. You were also reminded that you must be willing to reach out and use the resources available in your school environment. It is not possible to predict everything that may happen during the course of your life. It is certain that there will be times when you will have to make adjustments and important decisions because of situations over which you have no control. Your values, sense of personal power, decision-making skills, and ability to use assertive behavior are all valuable resources that you can rely on when you encounter socio-economic barriers or when unexpected events occur.

"If you are building a house and a nail breaks, do you stop building, or do you change the nail?"

- African Proverb

Images: WOMEN WHO

DONNETTE D. CHATTERS
TELECOMMUNICATIONS ANALYST

How would you feel if you had gone to your high school counselor for advice on choosing a career and, after glancing over your transcripts, he suggested several vocational schools with excellent secretarial programs? I suppose, if you had mentioned how much you enjoyed typing, advice of this sort would have been greatly appreciated. However, if you had different aspirations in mind—a college degree and a professional career—you may have thought the counselor's response was another way of saying, "Everyone is entitled to dream." That is what I thought about the situation. Nevertheless, I chose to attend college.

I enrolled in my first college class at a community college while I was still in high school. I was fully determined to show my counselor that I was not going to limit my dreams to a typewriter. I completed the course with a "B" and felt that I had gained a major victory over the "almighty test scores." Unfortunately, things did not go as well the following semester. As a result, I passed off my earlier academic achievement as sucker's luck and abandoned my dreams, for reality—work, marriage, children, divorce, and poverty.

I attempted to reenter college several times, but I lacked the confidence, the time, and the financial support that I needed in order to dedicate myself fully to schoolwork. Then something happened that turned my life around. A coworker received a tiny gold lapel pin for twenty-five years of state service as a typist. I suddenly realized that I had twenty-one more years to go! In my mind, I could see my old high school counselor's face glaring at me with an "I told you so" grin. I knew then that I had to make a decision as to where I wanted to spend my next twenty-one years.

I left my full-time civil service position and worked part-time for two years so that I could attend college. There were difficulties along the way; I had to rethink my decision more than once. However, I continued because I had a plan and realistic goals. Currently, I am completing work toward my degree in communication studies. In addition, I am employed full-time as a telecommunications analyst for the State of California.

Since my first attempt at attending college, I have learned that in order to succeed you must be motivated by yourself, for yourself, and in spite of yourself. Although your victories may be few and far between, they are yours to serve as reminders of successes yet to come.

OVERCAME ODDS

JOANNE LEWIS
UNIVERSITY ADMINISTRATOR

In my position as Assistant Vice Chancellor at the University of California, San Francisco, I am in charge of Facilities Management Services. I supervise a staff of approximately 250 people, who are responsible for all maintenance, renovation, and construction required for buildings owned and rented by the university.

On a typical day I attend as many as four or five meetings. I meet with other UCSF administrators as well as representatives of community organizations. I hold interviews with architects and contractors who wish to do business with UCSF. In addition, I meet with staff to review their work and to give them the guidance needed to do a job well.

I chose to be an administrator because I have the ability to pay attention to detail and to oversee several projects at the same time. I am skilled at organizing and directing the work activities of others. In addition, I enjoy working with people who have various backgrounds and abilities.

In high school I took business classes because my goal was a career in business. I wanted to be a secretary, so I worked hard in school and belonged to the Business Honor Society. I was so efficient that my teacher recommended me to type a manuscript while I was still a student. After completing the job, I knew I was a good typist because the work had been done professionally.

Perhaps I may have limited myself in some ways; I have always felt hampered by not having a college degree. Therefore, I felt that I had to work harder to succeed. Others encouraged and even pushed me and

showed me what I was capable of doing without a college degree. I have learned that there is little that can really limit me, except me. Of course, racism and sexism exist in this society and place limits on the society. Nevertheless, personal achievement is only limited by one's self and by access to information.

If I were to return to high school today, I would still want to have a career in business. However, I would take more college courses so that I would have a stronger background in business.

Career fields have changed enormously since I started working. No matter what your goals are, you must prepare yourself for the future which is now. Sample as many courses as you can while in high school. Prepare to complete some college courses to further develop your inborn talents. It is important to explore outside of what you already know. For example, knowing several languages can open up opportunities in the world of work. Do not limit yourself; learn as much as you can in every circumstance in which you find yourself.

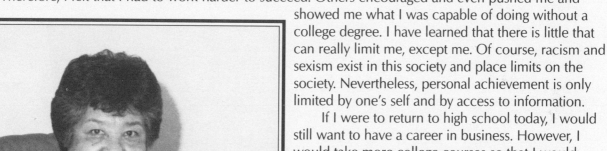

Chapter Seven

In its simplest terms, success is getting from point A to point B.

DEFINING MY OWN SUCCESS

Individual success results from the inner desire or motivation to achieve. Success occurs daily in life in many ways, great and small. There is no one set definition of success that fits every person and every situation.

- For a baby trying to learn how to walk, success is taking that first step.
- For a student struggling to pass a difficult course, success is getting a grade of C-.
- For a worker on a new job, success is getting the first paycheck.

During your career exploration you were introduced to a number of women who may be considered models for success. Each of these women has her own definition of success. Words and phrases that they used to describe themselves and their experiences reflect characteristics of success. Self-confidence, the ability to communicate, and creativity are examples of expressions that may be used to describe a successful person.

Go back to Chapter Five and review what the role models said to you. List phrases or statements that may be considered characteristics of success.

_____

_____

_____

_____

_____

_____

_____

_____

Select statements from your list and write a description of the successful Black woman.

_____

_____

_____

_____

_____

_____

_____

_____

Reaching for Your Own Star

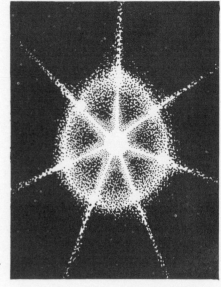

Your search for self has made you more aware of interests, skills, ideas, and ways of behaving that make you the unique person that you are. You have your own values, goals, and inner desire to achieve. You have the responsibility to set your own priorities and to decide what is important to you.

Write your definition of personal success.

_____

_____

_____

_____

_____

_____

_____

Your personal success will depend to a large extent on the kind of work you plan to do, the amount of money you expect to earn, and the help or support you expect to get from other people. In the long run, your ability to balance work, income, and resources will determine how well you meet your goals and measure up to your own standards for success.

> *"If you hitch your wagon to another person's star, you may never leave the ground."*
>
> **- Mattie Evans Gray**

Managing Income

The quality of your life-style will be greatly influenced by your ability to manage your income. This is a major responsibility, especially if others are depending on you for support. You are probably somewhat aware of this responsibility if you have worked part-time or on a summer job. What seems like a lot of money can be reduced to a few pennies unless you plan and spend wisely.

The model budgets that follow will provide you with an opportunity to try your hand at managing money. You will need to ask questions at home or do some research in the library in order to gather information about the costs of monthly expenses. Newspaper ads will also be helpful in determining the costs of housing, food, cars, and furniture.

Use the following information to prepare your model budgets.

Budget A:
You and one child live alone in an apartment. Your monthly income: AFDC—$475; child support—$50.

Budget B:
Both you and your husband work. You are buying a home and have one child. Your monthly income: take home pay—$2,350.

Budget C:
You live alone in an apartment. You are saving money to buy a car. Your monthly income: take home pay—$875.

MODEL BUDGET A

INCOME

Take-home pay .... _____
Social Security benefits.. _____
AFDC payments .... _____
Child support .... _____
Other income .... _____

Total: _____

EXPENSES

Housing
    Rent... _____
    Telephone.. _____
    Gas, electricity, water .... _____
    Household supplies .... _____
Food
    Groceries.. _____
    Outside meals.. _____
Clothing .... _____
Grooming and cosmetics .... _____
Medical
    Doctor.. _____
    Dentist.. _____
    Medicine and health aids .... _____
    Medical insurance .... _____
Transportation
    Car payment.. _____
    Gas, oil, upkeep .... _____
    Car insurance... _____
    Bus fare .... _____
Child care .... _____
Recreation
    Movies, sports, dances .... _____
    Hobbies.. _____
Church/Charity .... _____
Debts
    Credit card payments .... _____
    Installment payments .... _____
    Other loans.. _____
Other items.. _____
Savings... _____

Total: _____

Total income must equal total expenses.

MODEL BUDGET B

INCOME

Take-home pay .... _____
Social Security benefits .... _____
AFDC payments .... _____
Child support .... _____
Other income .... _____

Total: _____

EXPENSES

Housing
    Rent .... _____
    Telephone .... _____
    Gas, electricity, water .... _____
    Household supplies .... _____
Food
    Groceries .... _____
    Outside meals .... _____
Clothing .... _____
Grooming and cosmetics .... _____
Medical
    Doctor .... _____
    Dentist .... _____
    Medicine and health aids .... _____
    Medical insurance .... _____
Transportation
    Car payment .... _____
    Gas, oil, upkeep .... _____
    Car insurance .... _____
    Bus fare .... _____
Child care .... _____
Recreation
    Movies, sports, dances .... _____
    Hobbies .... _____
Church/Charity .... _____
Debts
    Credit card payments .... _____
    Installment payments .... _____
    Other loans .... _____
Other items .... _____
Savings .... _____

Total: _____

Total income must equal total expenses.

MODEL BUDGET C

INCOME

Take-home pay .... _____
Social Security benefits.. _____
AFDC payments .... _____
Child support .... _____
Other income .... _____

Total: _____

EXPENSES

Housing
    Rent... _____
    Telephone... _____
    Gas, electricity, water .... _____
    Household supplies .... _____
Food
    Groceries .... _____
    Outside meals.. _____
Clothing .... _____
Grooming and cosmetics .... _____
Medical
    Doctor .... _____
    Dentist.. _____
    Medicine and health aids .... _____
    Medical insurance .... _____
Transportation
    Car payment .... _____
    Gas, oil, upkeep .... _____
    Car insurance... _____
    Bus fare .... _____
Child care .... _____
Recreation
    Movies, sports, dances .... _____
    Hobbies.. _____
Church/Charity .... _____
Debts
    Credit card payments .... _____
    Installment payments .... _____
    Other loans.. _____
Other items... _____
Savings.. _____

Total: _____

Total income must equal total expenses.

My Budget Experiences

Was this an exciting learning experience? Was it frustrating? What did you learn about balancing income and expenses?

Write a brief summary:

_____

_____

_____

_____

•*My reaction to Budget A:* _____

_____

_____

•*My reaction to Budget B:* _____

_____

_____

•*My reaction to Budget C:* _____

_____

_____

Work, Income, Resources: Ingredients for Success

All of the role models discussed their work and how it has affected their lives. As you know, most of what you have written in your book has been related in some way to your preparation for entering the world of work. By now you should understand that what you are doing as a student will affect your future career.

You have identified the occupations that you are interested in, based on your skills, values, and the type of life-style that you desire. The quality of your life will be determined to a great extent by the level of your income. You will probably be in the workforce for about forty years, so you can expect to receive most of your income from the work that you do. That is one of the reasons why your decisions about work are so important.

There will likely be social and economic changes that may affect your employment and life-style. You have been made aware of some of these changes or unexpected events as well as the resources that you may need to use in order to adjust to these changes.

Although you must rely on your own abilities in order to reach your goals, it is also necessary for you to know when and how to involve others in your life and decisions. There are times when you must be dependent; you must be willing to seek guidance from parents, relatives, teachers, and others who are able to offer mature advice. Sometimes you must be interdependent; that is, you must work cooperatively with others to solve a problem or complete a task.

Personal Success: Goals and Action Plans

A goal is some specific thing that you want to do or some place or level that you want to reach. The knowledge of who you are provides you with an awareness of your potential; as a result, you are able to set realistic goals. You can reach your goals by following certain steps and by using your resources wisely.

In Chapter Six you were introduced to Diane who made some unwise decisions that resulted in her becoming a teenage mother. She could not return to school and graduate with her class, but that did not cause her to give up her goal of getting her high school diploma.

Review Diane's plan for reaching her goal and achieving personal success. Then project yourself into the future and set goals and develop plans for something you would like to achieve in one year, five years, and ten years. Later in life you can review your plans to see how well you were able to predict what you would do and how successful you were in reaching your goals.

DIANE'S GOAL AND ACTION PLAN

GOAL: To obtain my high school diploma within a year after my class graduates.

ACTION PLAN

THINGS I MUST DO:
1. Arrange child care
2. Enroll in school.
3. Get a part-time job.
4. Arrange schedule for time to take care of baby, work and study.
5. Work out financial arrangements with parents for handling my expenses.

MY RESOURCES:
Child Care: day care center and my grandmother.
Transportation: city bus and my parents' car.
Income: job at grocery store and my parents.
Leisure: my friends and church youth activities.

WHAT IF?

• If my job and my responsibilities as a mother cause me to take time away from my studies

• I plan to work out an arrangement with my grandmother to keep the baby two nights a week so that I can have time to study and catch up on my homework.

WHY I EXPECT TO REACH MY GOAL:

Because I am determined to get my diploma so I can find a job and earn money to support myself and my child.

PERSONAL SUCCESS: WHAT I EXPECT ONE YEAR FROM NOW

GOAL: _____

_____

ACTION PLAN
THINGS I MUST DO:

_____
_____
_____
_____
_____
_____
_____
_____
_____
_____

MY RESOURCES:

_____
_____
_____
_____
_____
_____
_____
_____

WHAT IF:
•*If* _____

_____

_____

•*I plan to* _____

_____

_____

WHY I EXPECT TO REACH MY GOAL:

_____
_____
_____

PERSONAL SUCCESS: WHAT I EXPECT FIVE YEARS FROM NOW

GOAL: _____

_____

ACTION PLAN
THINGS I MUST DO:

_____

_____

_____

_____

_____

_____

_____

_____

MY RESOURCES:

_____

_____

_____

_____

_____

_____

_____

WHAT IF:
•*If* _____

_____

_____

•*I plan to* _____

_____

_____

WHY I EXPECT TO REACH MY GOAL:

_____

_____

_____

PERSONAL SUCCESS: WHAT I EXPECT TEN YEARS FROM NOW

GOAL: _____

_____

ACTION PLAN
THINGS I MUST DO:

_____

_____

_____

_____

_____

_____

_____

_____

_____

_____

MY RESOURCES:

_____

_____

_____

_____

_____

_____

_____

_____

WHAT IF:
•*If* _____

_____

_____

•*I plan to* _____

_____

_____

WHY I EXPECT TO REACH MY GOAL:

_____

_____

_____

Who Am I?

When you began your search for self, you were probably wondering what you could learn that you did not already know. Now you have answered that question in many ways. This book is all about you—your values, interests, needs, skills, ideas, language behavior, motivation to achieve, career goals, and plans for the future.

ARE YOU THE PERSON YOU THOUGHT YOU WERE? _____

_____

_____

_____

WHAT DO YOU LIKE ABOUT YOURSELF? _____

_____

_____

_____

WHAT WOULD YOU LIKE TO CHANGE? _____

_____

_____

_____

WHY SHOULD OTHERS LIKE YOU? _____

_____

_____

_____

WHY SHOULD OTHERS DISLIKE YOU? _____

_____

_____

_____

Write an essay about yourself.

I Am

The Person I Am

This is your page. Use it to create a collage of photographs, drawings, and mementos that depict present and future **IMAGES** of you.

Advisory Committee

The writer expresses deep appreciation to each member of the committee for the expert guidance provided from the inception to the completion of *IMAGES*.

Sandra Clementin
> Coordinator, Displaced Workers Project, Oakland Private Industry Council

Gloria S. Curtis
> Director, Volunteer and Tutorial Programs, Los Angeles Unified School District

Charlene Diggs
> Vocational Education Staff Teacher, Compton Unified School District

Ida Johnson
> Special Programs Coordinator, Merced County Schools

Sandra Mack
> Associate Principal, Foothill High School, San Jose

Esther Nelson
> Sex Equity Coordinator, American River College, Sacramento

Valencia King Nelson
> President, Multicultural Youth and Family Systems, Santa Barbara

Dolores Ratcliffe
> President, Corita Communications, Inc., Los Angeles

Ceretha Sherrill
> Chairperson, English Department, Grant High School, Sacramento

Sara Thomas
> Vocational Testing and Counseling Consultant, Los Angeles

Joy Wigfall
> Psychiatrist, Sacramento

Acknowledgments

FOR HELPING TO MAKE THIS PROJECT A SUCCESS SPECIAL THANKS TO:

•Junior and senior high school students from the following cities for their ideas and candid comments:

Compton	Merced	Santa Barbara
Los Angeles	Oakland	San Jose
Lynwood	Sacramento	Ventura

•The twenty-one role models for graciously volunteering to become a part of *IMAGES*.

•Delores C. Datcher, Cheryl Brown Henderson, Juanita McDonald, and Thrisha Shriver for reviewing the manuscript.

•Mildred Hatcher for convening a student advisory group, Sacramento City Unified School District.

•Jacquelyn Snead, Los Angeles Unified School District, for assistance in developing the training and implementation module.

•Paula Heady for manuscript preparation.

•Hortense E. Thornton, CIRCLE Project Director, for unwavering moral support and for writing "Reading for Pleasure."

The following generously granted permission to use their material:

•From Lucille Clifton, permission to use poem number nine from *Good News About the Earth*. Copyright 1972, by Lucille Clifton.

•From National Academy Press, permission to adapt material from *High Schools and the Changing Workplace: The Employer's View*. Copyright 1984, National Academy Press.

•From Wade Nobles, permission to adapt portions of his lecture, "Reconstructing the Black Family," Sex-Equity Mini-Conference, Los Angeles, January 23, 1987.

•For valuable assistance and suggestions, thanks to Johnnie Mae Conner, Rose Crowder, Constance F. Gipson, Vincent Harris, Georgia Lee, Kathy Moore, Marianna Rivera, Milo Smith, Rick Vaughnes, Bettye O. Williams, Leona Williams, and Virginia Woods.

Credits

Editor, Carol Borden
Artistic Consultant, Edward Minor
Graphic Consultant, Sandra Honigsberg
Photographers:
Rick Diaz: Dixon, Ledbetter, Sklarek, Stevens
Sam Parsons: Bolden, Brown, Campbell, Crooks, Chatters, Farmon, Godbold,
    Lytle, McReynolds, Rhoe, Smith, Tanner, Weir
Bill Taylor: Hunnicutt, Lewis, Richardson, Spearman
Research Assistants: Nedra Evers, Colette Harris
Typography by Tempel Typographics

Index

88 78847

87-32 03-0135 300 11-88 20M